Fairy Tales for the New Age

By Arlene Williams

Illustrated by Joyce Rossi

The Waking Light Press
Sparks, Nevada

Printed in the United States of America
on recycled, acid-free paper
using soy ink

Library of Congress Catalog Card Number: 92-080607

Published by:

The Waking Light Press
P.O. Box 1329, Sparks, Nevada 89432

The Waking Light Press is an imprint of
Wee Smile Books

To the little child within who longs to discover those truths the world has left untaught. A.W.

To Lou for teaching me to believe in myself. J.R.

For dreams of dragons and magic —

Arlene Williams

Author's Note

These stories have grown from a desire to unite my deep love of fantasy with New Age concepts I have learned. In writing them, I have drawn on beloved fairy tale characters from my childhood, as well as used names and imaginary settings from a variety of cultures and races of people on this earth. However, no location is intended to be real and none of the stories are meant to represent any ethnic group of people or their heritage of myths.

Table of Contents

The Whisper Woman

Once there were two young princesses, named Dea and Yani, who lived in a castle high on a cliff above the sea. Every morning they woke to the cry of sea gulls circling far below. Yani would lay in bed, listening to their shrill song; but Dea would jump up and run to the window, looking for a glimpse of a ship upon the sea. However, the castle walls were so thick she could only see a tiny slice of shimmering water from her window, unless she leaned out far enough to see beyond the stone of the castle. Then Yani would pull her back and laugh at her for being so reckless.

"You're silly, Dea. Why can't you wait?" Yani said one morning. "Mother will take us to the sea today."

"I know," Dea answered with a frown, "But I like being the first one to spot a sailing ship."

"I like being the first one to finish my honey roll," Yani teased. Then she raced her sister along the stone corridors of the castle to get their breakfast.

It was mid-morning when the Queen led the sisters down the steep trail to her gardens. They were luxurious, filled with flowers and trees and shrubs

1

nestled on a ledge of the cliff overlooking the beach. Green vines cascaded over the edge like waterfalls, and potted plants hung everywhere from iron spikes drilled into the cliff face.

The girls played happily with their mother all morning, splashing in the surf below the gardens or sitting among the flowers watching ships upon the sea. Then, as they built a giant sand castle on the beach, the Queen grew tired. They went home without finishing it.

Later that day their mother fell ill with a fever. The next day and the next and the next, they did not go to the gardens by the sea. All that week the sisters played in their room, listening to the cry of the gulls and longing for their mother.

One morning they were told that a woman named Puna had come from the northern islands across the sea to take care of them. Dea was angry. She didn't want anyone to take the place of her mother. Yani, however, was curious. She had never met an islander.

"Don't talk to her," Dea whispered with a scowl as she watched the gray-haired woman walk toward them down the hall.

Yani ignored her sister. "Hello!" Yani called out. She ran to the woman and tugged on her sleeve. "You must be Puna. Did you bring me a present?"

"Yani! Hush!" Dea shouted.

Puna just chuckled. "Yes, I do have something.

It's for both of you. I just finished it."

Yani hurried Puna into their room, eager for the present. Dea followed slowly, not wanting to show any interest in it. However, she couldn't help but look cautiously over Puna's shoulder as the old woman searched through her worn travel bag for the gift.

"Here," Puna said happily. She pulled out a small piece of needlework framed in gold. "She's called the Whisper Woman. She has the power to heal and to help those in trouble. She's very, very special."

The two girls stared at a picture of a woman deep within the sea. Her skin looked green like the water. She stood among the tall, thin plants of kelp, stroking the fish around her like loving pets.

"Oh, she's beautiful," Yani said, reaching for the golden frame.

Puna handed Yani the fine yarn picture. The princess studied it closely, while her sister frowned impatiently beside her. Finally, Dea grabbed for it. "Let me see!" she whined. Then, all at once, Dea howled in pain. She raised her hand to find a sharp embroidery needle stuck into the end of her finger.

"Oh, goodness!" Puna said with dismay. "How could I have left that there?" She motioned for Dea to sit on her lap. "Come here, child. Come here."

Dea crawled into Puna's lap and felt the strong arms of the island woman fold gently around her. "Now close your eyes, Dea," said Puna. "I'll pull it out."

Dea closed her eyes and winced as the needle was removed. "It hurts," she moaned.

"Yes, and it's bleeding too." Puna nodded. "I know what we'll do. Let's call the Whisper Woman."

She paused for a moment, looking out beyond the window to the sea. Then she spoke, soft and slow, as if from far, far away. "Think of the sea, Dea. Yes, you must think of the sea. Breathe slowly... in and out, in and out. Hear your breath like the whisper of the sea upon the shore. Let your belly rise and fall like the waves. Soon she'll come to help you. Yes, she will... the Whisper Woman."

At first Dea tried to breathe slowly and deeply, but her sobs kept getting in the way. She felt angry, too, about Yani and Puna and the needle. Finally, she wriggled off Puna's lap. "No!" she shouted. "I don't want anyone but my mother to come."

The old woman watched her quietly with kind, brown eyes. She nodded with understanding. "Yes, I wish your mother could come."

Dea slumped in a chair and stared miserably at her sore finger. Everyone was silent. Then Yani asked, "Where does the Whisper Woman come from? What does she do?"

Puna touched the picture lovingly. "She lives near my island in a forest of kelp below the sea," explained Puna, "And when you call her with your deep, slow breath, she rides the waves to shore with her cloak of mist around her so no one can see."

"What does she do when she comes?" asked Yani.

"When she comes," said Puna very softly, "She wraps you in her mist and whispers to your pain or your fever or your fear. She tells your mind to grow strong and your pain to grow soft. She tells your body that it's time to heal."

"And you're not scared anymore?" asked Yani, wide-eyed. "And the hurt goes away?"

"Yes, it goes away," said Puna.

After that, when she was sick or hurt or afraid, Yani always called the Whisper Woman. She would curl up in Puna's lap, and together they would call with their deep, slow breathing. Soon the little princess would be sound asleep or playing happily again.

However, Dea would never call the woman in the sea. She knew the story wasn't true. If there really was a Whisper Woman, why was their mother still sick?

Dea spent more and more of her time alone, longing for the day when her mother would be well and they could go to the gardens to play by the sea. However, her mother grew worse with each new day, and Dea would slip away to the gardens by herself to walk among the flowers and cry.

One day, as Dea walked in the gardens, she heard someone coming along the path. Not wanting to be found, she climbed the tree beside her. It was a small, wind-swept pine that jutted out beyond the cliff. As she crawled along its trunk, she realized there was nothing beneath her but the beach far below.

The footsteps came and passed her by. It was the gardener and he hadn't seen her. She waited as she heard him whistle cheerfully and climb the path back to the castle. The whistling grew fainter and fainter until it disappeared altogether.

Then Dea caught sight of a ship far out at sea. She inched along the trunk a little more to get a clear view. It was a tall ship with red striped sails. There was a strange flag flying from its mast. She leaned forward, straining to see it. All at once, she felt a shudder as the tree gave way.

Dea screamed. She fell through the air with the tree as it dropped away from the cliff. Then the tree jolted to a stop. She turned her head in horror to see that all the roots but one had been ripped from their rocky crevices on the edge of the cliff. The tree dangled from one gnarled root, leaving her upside-down, clutching the tree trunk.

"Help!" she called to the gardener. "Help!" However, the gardener was gone, and no one else came; so she tried to inch back up the tree, but every movement set the pine swaying treacherously.

Her heart pounded in her chest as she stared at the beach far below. Her head began to spin, and a panic rose inside her that she could hardly control. She wanted to scream and scream and scream, but she was afraid the noise would somehow rip that root from its hold on the cliff.

There was nothing she could do but wait silently, in terror. And then, somewhere between the dizziness and the fear, she thought of the Whisper Woman.

So Dea began to breathe slowly, in and out, in and out. She felt her belly rise and fall, gently, like the sea. Slower and slower her breath came, until its rhythm matched the waves crashing on the shore again and again and again.

Soon Dea began to think of somewhere deep within the sea. It was a forest of kelp, filled with glinting schools of fish and an octopus and other creatures of the sea. There was a lady, too, as green as the water all around her. Her hair was long and wild. She was smiling and swimming up, up to the surface of the water.

Dea knew it was the Whisper Woman coming over the waves, now, hidden by the fog that crept to shore so quietly. She stood tall on the breakers as she rode them and whispered with a voice as gentle as the rumble of the surf, saying, "The peace. Feel the peace. Inside you, feel the peace."

The mist surrounded the cliff and the tree and Dea. Suddenly, the princess couldn't see the emptiness below her. There was nothing but her breath and the whisper of the sea. Then, all at once, Dea felt the touch of the Whisper Woman.

A long time passed as Dea clutched the tree trunk—awake, yet wrapped in softness like a dream. Then she heard the calls of Puna and Yani and the gardener. She answered joyfully, and soon she felt the strong arms of the gardener pulling up the pine and unwrapping her fingers from their grip around the tree.

Puna held her gently as Dea breathed softly, in and out, in and out. The old woman smiled. "You called the Whisper Woman," Puna said.

Dea nodded slightly. She looked out through the fog toward the sound of the sea. Then, quietly, she whispered, "And she came."

The next day Dea got permission from the King to visit her mother. A lady took her up the long flight of stairs to the Queen's quarters and opened the heavy jeweled doors. There sat her mother on the bed, looking pale but happy to see her.

"Mother!" Dea cried, rushing across the room.

The Queen opened up her arms to hug the princess, but suddenly she winced with pain.

"Does it hurt?" Dea asked her, trembling.

"A little," the Queen said.

"I know something that might help," Dea suggested. "I know a story."

Then Dea took her mother's hand and told her the story of the Whisper Woman.

The Children and the One

Long, long ago, in a village that was very poor, Gretchen and Karl lived with their mother and father in a small thatched hut. Though their life was hard, their parents always spoke to them with tenderness and taught them to look for the best in everything.

All year long the people of the village labored in the fields, growing wheat and barley for the Baron. The Baron owned the land they lived upon, and when the harvest came, the Baron's men would take most of the crop. Very little was left to store for the winter, so the village children collected wild fruits and nuts and roots from the forest each day for their families to eat.

One day the Baron's soldiers came to the village while Gretchen and Karl picked berries in the forest. The children cowered behind a rock, watching the soldiers shackle the people and burn down their small huts. Then the people were marched down the crumbling granite road that led to the Baron's castle.

"What are they doing? What do they want?" Karl cried as he stared after the knights on horseback.

Gretchen didn't answer him. Instead, she took her brother's hand and ran as fast as she could into the shelter of the forest.

Deeper and deeper, they made their way between the sturdy trunks of oaks and chestnut trees. They pushed through thickets and brambles, instead of following the paths, so they wouldn't be found by any hunters from the Baron's castle. When Karl got tired, Gretchen carried him on her back. Finally she could go no further. She gently set her brother down. "I think we're safe here," she whispered.

"I'm cold," Karl said with a shiver, but he knew they couldn't start a fire. The Baron's men might spot the smoke or see the light in the gray gloom.

"Stay here," Gretchen said as she wrapped her coarse, homespun shawl around him. Then she went to search for a place to hide and sleep.

Soon Karl and Gretchen were huddling in the hollow center of a giant chestnut tree. They had gathered some leaves from the forest floor to sleep on and found some clumps of dry moss to make a pillow for their head. There were chestnuts in the hollow hidden by a squirrel. The children ate them silently. Then Gretchen hummed softly to her brother.

"That reminds me of Mama singing us to sleep every night," said Karl sadly. "And I'm thinking of Papa, too, carrying me high on his shoulders so I can try to touch the stars."

12

"We'll see them again," said Gretchen. "We must have faith. We must remember what Mama always says about goodness. It is everywhere, even in the Baron's castle." She kissed her brother's forehead gently, just as their mother would have done. "Now go to sleep," she whispered.

It was the middle of the night when Gretchen and Karl woke. The chill was gone from their fingertips. A softness flowed through their tired muscles, making them warm all over. Then, all at once, a beautiful light shone about them.

Gretchen looked around in amazement. At first she thought it was a bright, full moon. Then she saw that the tiny hollow of the tree was filled with a sparkling sphere of light. It hovered silently above them.

"What are you?" asked Karl, half-afraid and half-delighted.

Gretchen reached out to touch the light. She felt a tingle in her fingers, and somehow, she could hear its answer. "It says," she told her brother, "It is called The One."

"One what?" asked Karl.

"I don't know." Gretchen shrugged. She touched it again. "But it must be good. It feels like... like Mama."

Karl touched it softly. "It feels like Papa, too."

Gretchen nodded. She was silent for a moment, listening with her fingertips as they probed the gentle

13

light. "And yet it is more than them, much more."

Karl smiled and yawned and settled back to watch the light. Soon both children were asleep, drifting in and out of dreams as The One floated above them. In the morning it was still there.

The children sat up in the hollow and stretched as best they could. They ate the last of the chestnuts; then they looked out at the brightness of the morning.

"What do we do?" asked Karl.

"I don't know." Gretchen shrugged, looking up at the light. "We could ask The One. Perhaps it knows."

She reached up and felt her fingers against the softness of the glow. Then she pulled back and looked at Karl in alarm. "It said to go to the castle."

"Not the castle." Karl shivered.

"Mama and Papa need us," Gretchen continued. "We must speak to the Baron."

"The Baron won't listen," Karl protested.

"The light will help us," Gretchen said, pointing to The One. "Mama and Papa need us. Touch the light and you'll know we have to go."

Karl touched the light. His fingers tingled softly. Suddenly he nodded in agreement. "Yes. I'll go," he said quietly.

Gretchen crept out of the hollow and listened carefully for any sounds of danger. Then the children moved back through the brambles and thickets the way they had come the day before. The ball of sparkling light followed them, hovering in the air above their heads.

Karl touched it again. "It helps me feel brave," he whispered.

Still, as they walked through the crisp autumn leaves on the forest floor, neither Gretchen nor Karl felt very brave. Ahead of them lay their burned out village and the long road to the Baron's castle.

"What does the Baron want with Mama and Papa and everyone?" Karl asked suddenly.

"The Baron is looking for something," Gretchen replied.

"What? A treasure?"

"No one knows." Gretchen shrugged. "It is something he dreamt of. They say it isn't real."

"But what does he want with Mama and Papa?" Karl repeated.

Gretchen shivered slightly in the shadow of a tree. "He dreamt he found what he was looking for while walking through our village. Ever since, he's had watchers spying and listening at windows. Mama thinks the Baron has gone mad from all the cruel things he's done. Perhaps he grew angry with the village, not finding what he wants, or perhaps he thinks the people keep it a secret from him."

"Maybe we can find what he's looking for, and he will let them go," Karl said hopefully.

Gretchen nodded and reached for her brother's

hand. "Perhaps," she said as they walked on.

It was midday when they came to the ruins of their village. Gretchen shivered in the emptiness that had been their home. Nothing stirred among the ashes except the wind. It seemed to whisper and taunt them. She reached up and touched the ball of light for comfort. All at once, the wind felt warm.

Then, searching the blackened ground, the children found a few polished stones, some bits of melted silver and one clay pot, nothing more. Gretchen put the stones and silver in the pot and set them on the ground.

"Shouldn't we bring them?" Karl asked.

Gretchen looked up toward the shimmer of the light. "That's not what the Baron is looking for," she answered as she turned to face the granite road. It curved up the hill and across the gray-green moor. "We'd better go," she said to her brother.

They started down the Baron's road, walking briskly with the wind to their back.

"I wonder why it's called The One? I wonder if it's magic?" Karl asked as they trudged along in the afternoon sun.

Gretchen shook her head. "It's more than magic. It's... It's..." she stammered but she couldn't put it into words.

Karl stretched upward to touch the light. "It's like a bit of everything," he said simply, "The wind and the birds—the trees and the people."

Gretchen nodded. "And Mama's sweet song and Papa's strong arms when he's hugging us."

"And fresh cut wheat and berry pie and the coolness of water at the spring," Karl sputtered with excitement.

"Yes." Gretchen smiled. "All those good things."

"I bet I know who it's not." Karl frowned.

"Who?"

"The Baron," Karl replied.

"Perhaps," Gretchen answered. "But isn't it called The One? Isn't it a bit of everything?" She grew silent as she listened to the crunch of the coarse granite gravel beneath her feet.

Halfway along the moor, the children were spotted by the Baron's men. They rode out from the castle on strong horses that thundered down the road. At first, Gretchen and her brother trembled at the sight of their gleaming armor and their swords. Then the shimmering circle of The One came close, touching the children, calming their fear.

"What is that?" asked the head of the castle guard, pointing suspiciously at the light.

"It is called The One," Gretchen answered. She spoke so strongly she surprised herself.

"What is it?" he asked sharply.

"It is what the Baron seeks," she said.

Karl looked at her in awe. "Really?" he whispered.

Gretchen squeezed his arm to silence him. The guard studied them carefully.

"What price do you demand for this... this thing?"

Gretchen summoned up her courage. "Freedom," she said, "For the prisoners from the village."

"Nothing more?"

"Nothing more," Gretchen replied.

"You're quite brave for a little brat," the guardsman said warily, "But come along. We'll let the Baron decide."

The Baron glared at Gretchen and Karl as they entered the great hall of the castle. The children looked around in awe at the rich tapestries and the tables piled with loaves of bread and wine and cheese and meat. There were ladies dressed in silk with rings of gold on their fingers. The Baron, himself, wore a blue velvet robe with ropes of pearls around his neck. The hollows of his eyes were darkened by the shadows of the room.

"What have you brought me?" the Baron asked the guard mockingly. "A pair of dirty children with a magic show?"

The guard looked hesitantly at the children, then he spoke. "The girl said this was what you sought for, my lord. I didn't want to overlook any possibility."

"Show me your magic then," the Baron demanded, pointing at the light.

"It is not magic," Gretchen answered calmly. "It is

more."

"More what?" the Baron roared.

"Come touch it and you will know," Gretchen answered.

The Baron rose up, stepping forward toward the light. He stopped halfway, his arm outstretched. He wanted to touch it, but he was afraid.

"It's a trick, isn't it? Some trick of wizardry? Some trap? I will not be tricked by a child," he yelled. "Tell me what this is."

Suddenly Karl spoke up. "It is the good," he explained. "It is the good in everything."

"Foolishness." The angry man spat at the boy. Then he pointed to the head guardsman. "Take them. Throw the children in the dungeon with the rest of them." He turned away, then turned back to stare at the sphere of light. "But make them leave this thing with me."

The children were chained together and shoved down a long winding stair toward the darkness of the dungeon. Karl broke into tears. "It didn't help," he said again and again. "The One said it would help us. It didn't."

"Don't worry," said Gretchen. "Soon we'll be with Mama and Papa." Then, in the gloom of the stairway, she pointed to a faint glow following them like a shadow. "See," she whispered. "It has not left us. The light is here, as well as back there. You just must look harder to see it."

Karl nodded. A smile flickered across his face.

Gretchen smiled back. "Remember—the good is everywhere."

Soon the dungeon door clanged shut behind them; but even in that rank darkness, Gretchen felt the comfort of The One, like a softness deep within, as she hugged her mother and father tight.

However, the dungeon was still a very fearful place for the others from the village. There was little to eat, and the rats scared the smallest children so they cried out in their sleep. Over and over again, to calm them, Gretchen told the people the story of The One. Soon they began to believe her. Some could even see that shadow of the light following her wherever she went.

The children saw it the clearest. They jumped up high to touch what they could barely see, and when they did, they felt a tingle in their fingertips. Then they would all shout, "It's coming. We feel it. It's coming."

Gretchen would nod and smile. "Something will happen," she would say, "Very soon."

In little more than a week, the Baron came to the dungeon door. "Where is she?" he called to the jailer. "Where is that little witch?"

Gretchen waited by the door. Slowly, the key clicked in the lock. The door squealed as it opened.

There stood the Baron, frowning miserably, with the shimmering light of The One above his head.

"You have cursed me," he hollered. "Stop this wicked thing or I will burn you for a witch."

Gretchen curtsied deeply. "I've only brought what you truly seek," she replied. "It is the good in you."

The Baron wasn't listening. "It follows me everywhere, daring me to touch it. I won't," he swore. "I won't."

Gretchen calmly repeated, "It is the good in you." She reached up and touched the shimmering light. "It can not harm," she explained. "It is only good."

Now the Baron was crying, sobbing, pleading with her. "Take it from me," he begged. "I can not sleep. I can not eat. Make it go away."

"I will show you," Gretchen said. She took his hand in hers and placed it over his own heart. "Feel it. There is good in you. I know there is. I know it."

"No." The Baron shook his head.

Then Gretchen smiled and looked him in the eye. She saw fear there, and hope. "Yes," she said simply. "Yes, there is."

The Baron looked at her, trembling. He reached up toward the shimmering light. This time he touched it; and as he did, the light traveled down his arm, surrounding him. It sparkled and spread until it filled every corner of the dungeon and everyone in it. Even the rats were radiant with joy.

21

The Baron stood a moment, transformed with the happiness he felt. Then the light was gone. That wonderful sphere vanished. The Baron looked at the child before him with dismay, but Gretchen shook her head and smiled.

She curtsied again. "It's in your eyes, my lord."

"Yes," he cried incredulously. He smiled, his eyes sparkling with a vivid light. "And I see it in your eyes, too."

Then, turning to the people, he bowed his head in apology. In the torchlight, Gretchen saw a tear escape down his cheek and drop to the floor. "You can go," he said softly. "You are free."

Gretchen touched his tunic tenderly, answering, "And so are you."

That night, in the great hall, a jubilant celebration took place. The Baron pledged to rebuild the ruined village and share his riches with all the people. Then, as the soldiers and the villagers and the noble men and ladies danced and ate and sang, the people pledged to keep him as their lord.

No one danced harder than Gretchen and Karl. The children twirled in dizzy circles. They hugged and kissed their mother and father a hundred times. They tasted everything the Baron's cooks had laid out on the tables.

"I will miss it. I will miss that beautiful light," Karl whispered between mouthfuls of sweet strudel and

22

honey cake.

"It isn't gone," Gretchen whispered back.

"That's right," Karl agreed as he looked around him at the people's happy faces. "It isn't gone." He glanced up at the Baron and waved.

Gretchen looked at the Baron too. In the torch-light, she saw a faint halo of light around his head. Then she watched her mother and father dancing in the firelight. "It's like Mama always told us," she said joyfully. "The good is everywhere and it's never gone."

The Whistle and the Rain

This is the story of a magic whistle and the boy, Keevon, who lost it. It happened long ago in a kingdom called Tarrizon where it rained very little. What rain did fall, raced down the mountains and hills of the land barely soaking the hard-baked earth. Only the slow-melting winter snow on the high peaks could nourish the mountain forest and feed the deep springs in the desert where Keevon lived.

All summer long the farmers of Tarrizon worked the forests of lum trees on the mountaintops, gathering wood for the winter. Keevon and his father were among them. Once a week, in their old farm wagon, they would go up the mountain high above their home to cut trees. Keevon loved to go, even though the work was hard, just to feel the cool mountain air and hear the whistle of birds in the forest.

One day, as Keevon chopped wood with his father among the trees, he watched the sky anxiously for rain. Earlier that morning he had left his little whistle by the dry creek bed farther down the valley. He had laid it on a rock in the sunshine but forgot it when his father called him back to the wagon.

Now his whistle pouch was empty, which bothered him greatly. The whistle had been Grandfather's. It was old and special. Magically, it called the birds to him. He didn't want to lose it to the rain.

The boy begged his father for a chance to return to the creek bed and save the whistle, but the big man just worked on and on. "Snow can come early to the mountains," his father told him as he split the rounds of wood. "There isn't time to worry about whistles today."

"But it's Grandfather's whistle," Keevon protested. "It's all I have of him. I can't lose it, too."

"Every loss brings gain, eventually," his father said firmly. "Now get to work, Keevon."

Thinking of Grandfather, Keevon stacked the wagon with wood. Grandfather had known every type of bird living on this mountain. Keevon knew them too. Each bird had a secret name Grandfather had taught him. Each one was a friend.

"Karutha," Keevon whispered. "Mallos. Keenon. Shouvee. Letos. Brias. Tawn. Chuna...." Keevon repeated those secret names as he worked, calling on his friends, the birds, to keep away the rain and protect the whistle.

That afternoon thunderclouds rolled toward the mountain top. They churned and rumbled through the air as Keevon frowned. Soon the wind roared through

26

the tiny mountain valley. The rain came blasting down as each drop rolled off those rocky slopes toward the desert below.

Keevon stood in the pouring rain, glaring at the clouds. He felt a coldness grip his heart. In the stream bed down the valley, Keevon knew the water was rising, taking with it Grandfather's special gift.

Then, all at once, Keevon felt like a thundercloud inside. He turned to his father and shouted, "It's gone! It's gone and I hate you."

Keevon's father stared back silently, not knowing what to say. Finally, realizing the mistake he had made, the man touched his son's shoulder and said, "I'm sorry, Keevon. I really am. We'll stop at the creek on the way home. We'll find it."

But Keevon turned away. "It's too late now," the boy said. "Too late to be sorry." Then Keevon sat miserably beneath a large lum tree, watching the rain.

When the storm ended, Keevon's father finished cutting up the last tree for the day. They loaded the wagon together; then Keevon climbed silently to the wooden seat behind the horse. Keevon's father nudged the reins and the old horse started down the mountain.

Soon they forded the creek. It gushed with water. Keevon saw his father look around hopelessly at the rain swollen stream. The man shook his head regretfully and turned to Keevon.

Keevon looked away. He had no hope, now, that

the whistle could be found. He stared angrily at the road ahead and didn't say a word all that long ride home.

Autumn came and Keevon drove up the mountain with his father for the last wagon load of wood. The mountains felt empty. Only a Torhawk, soaring high above the valley, called to him as they circled up, up through the lum forest.

Everything had changed since that summer storm. Without the whistle, Grandfather's magic vanished and so had Keevon's smile. Keevon barely spoke to his father anymore, and his anger grew with every thought he had of the whistle.

So Keevon sat silently beside his father, now, feeling numb and distant. His father looked at him uneasily and cleared his throat. "I've been remembering that whistle of Grandfather's," the man said hesitantly. "It would be fairly easy to make another."

Keevon turned away.

"I could make it for you or show you how. When I was a boy, I watched your grandfather make many whistles."

Keevon was silent. Then he turned toward his father. For a moment, Keevon saw the pain in his father's eyes, but that didn't stop him from lashing out. "The magic's gone! The whistle's gone!" Keevon shouted. "No one can make another. Not you! Not me! No one!"

Keevon saw his father wince. "Stop it!" the man yelled. "For Grandfather's sake, stop it!"

But Keevon turned away again and watched the dust rise behind them on the road.

A little further on, Keevon's father slowed the wagon and tried again. "When I was a boy, we barely had enough to eat," he explained. "Your grandfather was a good, kind father to me; but he was a dreamer, not a farmer. He was always watching birds, and every year the gasha harvest was poor."

"No!" shouted Keevon. "I won't listen to you. You never loved the birds. You never learned their names. You hate his magic and I won't listen."

"I was too busy trying to make the gasha plants grow to think of birds," replied Keevon's father.

However, Keevon still wouldn't listen. He covered his ears and his father fell silent. The wagon creaked as it lurched forward up the road.

Then, as they crossed the dry stream bed, Keevon saw an old man sitting on its bank, cleaning the dirt from something in his hands. His clothes were wrinkled and torn. A small bundle hung from his shoulder. He was a Dirfna, a wandering man.

The man put his hands to his lips and blew into something small and wooden. Keevon heard a faint note. He jumped. It was his whistle. He knew it was, for there was a bird flying low around the Dirfna man.

The old man blew another note, and the bird

29

landed on his bundle bag. Another bird settled on the man's boot as a glow spread across his travel-weary face, touched now by the magic of the whistle.

"That old man has your whistle," Keevon's father said, stopping the wagon.

Keevon didn't move. He just stared at the whistle. His father put down the horse's reins and shifted his weight to climb out of the wagon. In a minute, Keevon knew, his father would buy back the whistle, and then Keevon would have to forgive his father for letting the whistle get lost.

Keevon hesitated a moment, wanting the whistle. However the anger in Keevon's heart was strong. It wasn't willing, yet, to be let go. All at once, Keevon turned to his father and shook his head. "What whistle?" Keevon said coldly. "I have no whistle, remember? My whistle is gone, like Grandfather."

"It's your whistle," Keevon's father repeated.

Keevon felt a quiver in his throat. His lip trembled. However, he still shook his head. "No!"

His father closed his eyes and sighed. Finally he said, "Have it your way, Keevon." Then the man picked up the reins, and the wagon rumbled across the creek bed, up the dusty road.

The next morning Keevon woke with an ache in his heart. He gazed beyond the doorway of his family's small mud house to the broad, flat desert that stretched to the empty north. The boy pulled on his tunic and walked toward that openness, thinking of the whistle.

At the edge of a ravine, Keevon sat on a rock and stared at the sky. Thunderclouds skittered toward him. Lightning flashed on the horizon. Keevon didn't care. He only cared about the whistle. He should have taken it from that dusty old man, but he had been so angry with his father.

And then, just as he thought of his father, he felt a hand on his shoulder. "I have a piece of wood for you," said a voice, his father's voice, from behind. "It's the right size and shape. It would make a good whistle."

Keevon stared out beyond the ravine, silent. His father laid the wood at his feet and left without another word. Keevon watched the lightning flash in the distance. Then he put his head in his arms and cried.

Eventually, shadows fell across Keevon as thunderclouds filled the sky, but Keevon didn't look up until the rain drops fell. Then a bird caught his eye. It was a small plain bird that blended with the dusty desert browns. Keevon called to it by its special name.

"Karutha," said Keevon softly.

The bird didn't come. It didn't leave either. It settled in a bush, sheltered from the rain, watching him.

"Karutha," Keevon said again, but still the bird didn't come.

31

Keevon shivered in his rain-soaked tunic. He looked at the blackened sky. He wished Grandfather could come down from the clouds and give him another whistle, but that could never happen. Grandfather was gone forever.

Then Keevon looked down and saw the wood at his feet. It was a small, knobby piece of wood that reminded him of Grandfather's whistle. "Can there really be another whistle?" Keevon asked himself. "Can Grandfather's magic still be here?"

Keevon picked it up and felt for his knife in its sheath at his side. "I will show him," Keevon said, thinking with defiance of his father. "I will show him I can make a whistle."

Keevon dug the knife's blade into the wood. A chunk broke off. Then he made another gash on the other side. Keevon frowned. He wasn't sure if this was the right way to make a whistle.

And then there was another rustle in the bush. Keevon looked up. A second bird watched him.

"Karutha," Keevon whispered, knowing the bird wouldn't come. He looked at the sky. He wanted so much to have a whistle. Then, suddenly, he thought of the day his grandfather died.

All at once, a great trembling sob flowed through him. He put down the knife and let the wood slip from his hand. How could he carve a magic whistle without Grandfather by his side? The longing within him welled up and spilled forth as he called to the emptiness around him. "Grandfather!" he cried. "Grandfather!"

There was no answer. However, the wind subsided and Keevon knew something had changed. Perhaps his grandfather wasn't lost forever. Keevon felt him near. He stood up to scan the desert, hoping to somehow see Grandfather.

He saw, instead, his father standing on a high rock far away, watching silently. He looked so small to Keevon. He could have been a young boy Keevon's age, looking out across the desert at Grandfather talking with the birds.

Yes. Keevon saw his father, now. He saw a young boy who had to work hard to help the family. He saw a boy who didn't have time to love the birds. Keevon knew what his father had said was true. As long as Keevon could remember, Grandfather had never worked the farm. Grandfather had always spent his time teaching Keevon about the birds.

In the distance, Keevon's father raised his hand and waved. Keevon hesitated a moment, then raised his own hand and waved back. He wanted to call out to his father, to have him come back and show how to shape the whistle. Just then, though, the man disappeared, going back to the farm to work with the gasha plants.

Keevon looked after him sadly, wondering what would have happened if he could have forgiven his father that first day. Perhaps his father would have carved a whistle and learned Grandfather's magic. Perhaps they'd be spending their evenings together, walking with the birds.

Then Keevon shook his head and smiled, knowing that his father could never carve the whistle, just as Grandfather could never farm. His father didn't know the magic—he only knew the gasha plants. His father was the farmer, and the carving of the whistle was left for Keevon.

So Keevon picked up the knife and the wood and began again. This time he thought of his grandfather calling the birds and the birds flocking to him. He still didn't know how to make a whistle, but he felt his grandfather's magic.

The raindrops fell softly, now. A third bird flew to the bush. Keevon smiled. Grandfather always told him that magic came in threes. He stared at the bird. He felt Grandfather very near.

"Grandfather," he said calmly. "I know you are with me. I think perhaps these birds know, too."

The raindrops stopped. Keevon kept working. "Karutha," Keevon whispered. "Mallos. Keenon. Shouvee. Letos. Brias. Tawn...." Over and over again, he repeated the names of all the birds Grandfather had taught him as he carved the magic whistle.

Soon the sun broke through the clouds, warming Keevon's back. He kept on working as the whistle formed. It was crude. It needed sanding. It didn't look at all like Grandfather's whistle, not yet.

Then Keevon put it to his lips and blew. He watched the birds. They fluttered their wings briefly. He blew again a little harder. Suddenly the birds took flight.

They circled high above him. He thought they were gone. Then one settled on his shoulder and another on his knee. The last bird landed on his outstretched finger.

"Hello, my friends," he whispered softly. "Karutha."

Unicorn Birthday

On the shores of Lake Wisdom, long, long ago, a young servant girl named Tanna woke with the rising sun. She sat up on her small cot in the pantry of the royal castle and rubbed her sleepy eyes. Then she jumped to her feet and looked toward the kitchen, wondering if anyone would remember it was her birthday.

Quickly, she dressed and went to the kitchen to help the cook with the fire. As she bent down to add another log to the blaze, Cook shook a finger at her.

"Not today, Tanna." Cook said. "It's your tenth birthday."

Tanna looked up, joyfully. "You mean it's true?" she asked. "You mean it's true about your tenth birthday, even for me?"

"Certainly," said Cook, pointing to the proclamation tacked to the kitchen door. "Tanna Yerrling to appear before the Wizard of the Isle this twentieth of May at eight o'clock," read Cook. "Hurry now or you'll be late."

Cook sat the girl down before an old cracked

bowl full of porridge. Then she went about her duties preparing breakfast for the King and the Queen and Prince Jonz.

Tanna ate her porridge as she stared dreamily at the pots and pans already piled high in the wash tub. She watched Cook stir fresh berries into the creamy batter for the King's oat cakes. She gazed outside the window at a chore boy carrying water from the well. However, she barely noticed him or the cook or the dishes; for her thoughts were already miles away, lost in her visions of Wizard Isle.

"Tanna," Cook spoke firmly as she poured the batter into tins, "The ferryman leaves at seven sharp."

Tanna jumped. She ran to comb her hair and wash in her little pantry basin. As she scrubbed her face she whispered to her reflection in the water, "The magic will work for me. I know it."

However, just as she turned to leave for the ferry, she saw a mouse watching her from beneath the blanket on her cot. Tanna shuddered and shouted as she waved her arms furiously, "Scoot! Go!"

The mouse jumped off the cot and disappeared into a bin of onions. Tanna looked toward her blanket where he had hidden. She shivered. Suddenly, she wished she could leave behind, forever, this life as a servant girl.

"Tanna!" Cook yelled sternly from the kitchen, "You haven't long to catch the ferry."

"I'm going," Tanna called as she rushed for the door. Then she ran like the wind down the road to the dock.

She reached the dock in time to see the ferryman coming toward her across the lake on his raft. She looked beyond him to Wizard Isle looming mysteriously above the mist. The sight of it made her tremble with excitement.

And then she heard the clip, clop of horses hooves. Startled, she turned to see the royal coach stopping right before her. The carriage door was opened by the footman, and Prince Jonz stepped down. Tanna curtsied deeply. She was afraid to look up.

"Is it your birthday too?" asked the Prince with surprise.

"Yes, Your Highness," Tanna mumbled.

"Well, let me take your hand," said the Prince kindly. He grabbed her hand and helped her up, but she kept her head bowed meekly.

Prince Jonz strode toward the edge of the dock. "What a glorious day," he shouted. "I know the magic will work for me. I can feel it."

Tanna was surprised. "Of course the magic will work for you, Your Highness," she said politely. "You're a prince. It must work for you."

Prince Jonz turned to look at her. "Oh, no. That's Wizard Isle, and the magic there is much older than kings and queens and princes. It's deep and it's pure. I have no power over it just because I'm the Prince."

Tanna bit her lip. She stared at the deep green of the island, wondering whether she had any chance to make the magic work if even a prince could not control it.

Then, before the ferryman reached the dock, another boy appeared. Tanna's hopes tumbled. Now she would have to share the magic among three. She looked at Wizard Isle, desperately hoping there would be enough magic for all of them and she would not be forgotten.

The boy bowed before the Prince and introduced himself. He was a farm boy, named Rappo, from the western shore of Lake Wisdom. His clothes and hands were stained with dirt from working the fields. He looked silently at the sky.

"What do you see up there?" asked the Prince.

Rappo bowed his head slightly. "I watch for eagles, Your Highness."

"Eagles?"

"Yes, Your Highness." The boy glanced up at Wizard Isle and sighed. "I work in the fields day after day after day. But this day, my tenth birthday, I long to be free of the earth... to fly."

The Prince smiled to himself. "Yes, of course. I understand. I, too, long for a change. I long to be—"

The ferryman interrupted him. "Ready yourselves," the man called as his raft reached the dock. "Prepare for Wizard Isle."

Tanna and Rappo waited as Prince Jonz stepped aboard the log raft. Then the ferryman motioned for Tanna and the farm boy to board.

On the crossing, Tanna felt giddy with excitement and fright. She had never been on Lake Wisdom before. As a servant girl, the only water she was allowed near was the dish water and laundry water and scrub water for washing tables and floors.

Tanna watched the waves come rolling toward her until her stomach turned a somersault. Then, with a deep breath, she stared across the lake toward the castle. It grew smaller and smaller as, slowly, her dreary world as a servant began to fade.

When they reached Wizard Isle, the children climbed onto the dock and waited silently in front of a little stone hut. All at once, the bell of the royal chapel on the mainland sent eight chimes ringing across the water. The door creaked open. A very short, very plump little man stepped out.

"Tanna Yerrling," he said.

Tanna was surprised at the strength of his voice. He looked so old and so small. She nodded and he cleared his throat.

"Come forward," he told her.

Tanna stepped forward nervously, not wanting to. She thought that the Prince should be first, or at least the farm boy. She bent down before the little man as

41

he placed a hand atop her head.

Instantly, she felt very still. She looked up. The old man winked at her kindly, and Tanna felt hopeful in her heart that the magic would work for her after all.

Then Rappo knelt down before him and, finally, Prince Jonz. Tanna marveled that the Prince didn't mind at all being last. He was as cheerful as when she first saw him on the dock.

"I am the Wizard of the Isle," announced the man. "Follow me."

He turned toward a stone path that led up the hill toward the top of the Isle. Tanna's eyes grew wide as they passed the magic gardens of blue bells and coral bells, which chimed musically with the breeze. There were groves of oaks and aspens holding whispered conversations, and a little brook chattering noisily as it tumbled past them downstream.

Soon they reached a circular stone ruin. There were twelve ancient marble columns dressed in lichens of red and green and gray. Some columns tipped sideways. Others balanced broken blocks of marble precariously in the air.

In the center of the ruin, hung the tapestries. Tanna had never seen anything like them in her life. There were three. The first one was of a golden eagle. The second was of a unicorn. The last was a tapestry of a tiny gray mouse.

The wizard stopped before the tapestries. He cleared his throat again and began, "Today is your tenth birthday, and for a little while today, you have the chance to become one of the creatures you see here. Pick the one which in your heart you long to be, but remember, only one of you can be the eagle and only one of you the unicorn and only one the mouse."

Tanna's gaze went immediately to the tapestry of the unicorn. It stood before her in purity and grace. Its legs were built for speed and power and glory. Its head was noble, and its eyes were bold and wise and free. In her heart, she knew the unicorn was what she longed to be.

Then the jet black eyes of the mouse caught hers. A fear rose within her. She thought of the mouse she saw that morning on her cot. She shook her head. She could never be a mouse. She detested mice. She hated the way they scuttled through the kitchen at night, searching for crumbs.

The wizard came close to Tanna, now, and put a hand on her shoulder. He stared deeply into her eyes as if he knew what she was thinking. "However, there will be no magic unless you can shape it from within," he said. "So you must look to your feelings, and be what you long to be in your mind and your heart and your dreams. Only then will the magic work. Only then can you be what you really want to be."

The wizard winked at her and walked to the edge

of the ruin. Suddenly, he vanished.

Tanna stared blankly at the spot where the wizard had been. Then she looked sadly back toward the tapestries. Tears filled her eyes; for she knew, when she looked inside herself, she didn't feel like the unicorn.

She sat on a fallen block of stone, closing her eyes as the tears flowed from them. She wiped them back, but it was no use. Inside, she felt like a little gray mouse hiding from the world. Tanna cringed. What if the magic turned her into one?

And then she heard someone move across the stones in front of her. She opened her eyes to see Rappo, the farm boy, running up the hill. At the top he became the golden eagle soaring off above the trees.

"Yes, Rappo is the eagle," Tanna murmured.

She looked around for the prince. He stood behind her, staring at the tapestries. Tanna curtsied deeply. "Your Highness, the unicorn is for you. I will not try to take it from you. I haven't the heart for it."

Prince Jonz turned to look at her with a puzzled smile. Then he laughed. "Ah, but you want it, don't you?"

Tanna winced and bowed her head.

"Yes. You want to be the unicorn," the Prince repeated. "And you must try. I will not take my turn until you've taken yours."

"Oh, no," Tanna protested. "You go first. It's not proper for a prince to be last."

"It's proper for a prince to be obeyed," said Prince Jonz, "And I command you to go first."

Tanna looked up at him in horror. "But I can't. If I were to take the unicorn, you would be left with the mouse."

"That's true," said Prince Jonz thoughtfully, "Then... I know! You must help me become the unicorn."

"Oh, yes," said Tanna gratefully, "I will. Yes."

"Come here," commanded the Prince, pointing to a spot before the tapestries. "We will both kneel here and I will close my eyes. I have a poor imagination, you see, so you will describe every detail of the unicorn. Then I will be able to picture it in my mind, and the magic will work for me."

Tanna knelt beside the Prince and turned toward the tapestry. She studied the image of the creature—standing proud in a green meadow, watching gray clouds beyond the distant hills. Tanna knew it was only a picture woven of colored thread, but as she looked at the unicorn with love in her heart, she felt it would come alive any moment.

"The unicorn is bold and sleek," she began. "White as the purest snow. It looks like a horse—but more powerful and wise."

45

"Touch the cloth," urged the Prince. "Describe everything."

Tanna's spine tingled as she reached out to touch the cloth. It tickled her fingertips with its softness. "It is smooth," she said happily, "And thick like the coat of the unicorn. It smells like a fresh green meadow with the scent of rain in the wind."

"The horn," prompted Prince Jonz. "Help me see the horn."

"The horn, it almost gleams," Tanna whispered. "Yes. It gleams, with every spiral perfect as it reaches toward the sky."

"Now the eyes," said the Prince. "Tell me about the eyes."

"Oh, the eyes..." Tanna murmured. "The eyes..."

She stared at the unicorn's eyes. They were kind. They were strong. They drew her into them as she imagined the wind in the unicorn's mane and heard hooves pounding the earth. Then she saw herself as the unicorn—galloping through the forest shadows, splashing across a cold, clear stream. For a brief moment, she felt like the unicorn, pure and free.

"Yes," she whispered breathlessly. "Yes."

And then she blinked and looked around her. She stood on the shore of Lake Wisdom, looking out beyond the island toward the castle on the other shore. She barely remembered what it was.

She watched the sky for several minutes, feeling

confused and very strange. At last she looked down at her long, slender white legs. She found she had four hooves and an incredible desire to race with the wind. All at once, Tanna realized she was a unicorn.

She stood for a moment with her head held high, listening to the waves wash gently onto the shore. She felt a power in her heart and the shiver of magic running through her horn. Then she turned and charged into the forest.

Back among the ruins on the hillside, she looked for the Prince, but he had vanished. Then, high on the hilltop, she saw a little gray mouse watching her intently from a rocky outcrop. She trotted up to him. She knew he was Prince Jonz.

The mouse sat up on his hind legs and twitched his whiskers merrily. She looked at him silently, for a long while, then bent down to touch his head gently with the very tip of her horn. The mouse winked at her and bowed deeply. Then he disappeared into a hole beneath the rock and was gone.

It was hours later when Tanna found herself, human again, chewing meadow grass beside a clear green pond. She laughed and spat out the grass, then looked around her at the deepening shadows of the island. Someone was coming toward her through the trees. It was the Prince.

Tanna ran up to him and kneeled on the ground before him. "Forgive me, Your Highness," she apologized. "I don't know why it happened. If I had known how the magic worked, I would have gladly become the mouse, so you could have been the unicorn."

"Tanna," said the Prince, "I had no wish to be the unicorn."

"That's not true," Tanna argued. "You asked me to help you imagine one."

"Yes, I did," agreed Prince Jonz. "But just so the magic could work for you. You see, all along, I really wanted to be the mouse."

"The mouse?" Tanna stammered, "Oh no, Your Highness. You couldn't have wanted to be a mouse. You're the Prince."

The Prince took Tanna by the hand and helped her up. "Don't you see?" he asked jubilantly. "The mouse is what I wanted to be—small, insignificant, hiding in the tiniest of places so no one could find me."

Tanna looked at him, bewildered.

"Where can a prince go to hide in this kingdom?" he continued. "When is a prince not on parade? When is he unimportant? Just a boy? Just me?" The Prince sat on a rock and sighed. "But for these few hours as a mouse, I was ordinary. I was free."

Tanna stood silent for a moment. Then she nodded. "I do see," she said softly. "And it will be a secret between us... just you and me."

Quietly, the Prince and Tanna walked back

48

through the magic gardens and groves of the island to the dock where Rappo was waiting with the ferryman. They greeted him with a silent nod and stepped aboard the raft. None of them spoke on the journey back across the water. They just stared as the island grew smaller and smaller in the afternoon light, remembering how their day had been.

Then, when they reached land once more, Rappo smiled. "Nothing will ever be the same," he said simply.

Prince Jonz grinned in agreement. He climbed into the carriage that was waiting for him. "Yes. Everything has changed," he said with a happy nod.

All at once, the carriage took off toward the castle and the farm boy disappeared down the road, leaving Tanna alone to watch the ferry slowly make its way back to Wizard Isle.

As she watched, she smiled to herself, understanding what Rappo and the Prince had meant. Tonight, she knew, she would eat the same old porridge in the same cracked bowl and wash the stone floor of the kitchen by moonlight, yet it wouldn't be the same for the unicorn's magic was still with her.

Finally Tanna turned from the dock and walked to the castle, humming a cheerful tune. It wasn't long before she stood at the open kitchen door, staring at the dirty plates stacked high in the wash tub. She thought one last time of Wizard Isle; then she stepped through the doorway with her head held high, ready to be a servant girl once more.

Cook greeted her merrily from the hearth, pointing out the dish tub to Tanna. Tanna strode to it calmly. She sunk her hands deep into the water, chatting with Cook as she washed the plates and cups and spoons. For the first time in her life, she enjoyed doing dishes, for now she worked with the strength and grace of a unicorn.

Finding a greasy spoon marked with the initials of the Prince, she washed it carefully. She thought of tonight, how those pantry mice would scamper across the floor while she lay on her little cot in the darkness. Tanna smiled, knowing she would think kindly of them from now on, all because of the Prince.

Lovingly, Tanna dried the silver spoon and laid it in the cupboard. Then she picked up a new spoon, humming softly, not minding how many were still left to wash. Finally she stopped to gaze at her little cot in the pantry. She felt a joy within her, knowing tonight, when she closed her eyes to sleep, she would gallop again as a unicorn through her dreams.

The Flight of Angels

Once upon a time, on a fluffy, puffy cloud, there was a little one-room school for angels. Every morning eight little angels would rise from their white cloud beds, smooth their robes, and meet in front of the school to wait for Hugh, their instructor. And every morning, when Hugh had opened the school house door, the angels would sing a song of glory as the sun rose.

At least it was supposed to be a song of glory, but the little angels either sang off-key or forgot the words or were busy making faces at the teacher behind his back. The only little angel who sang perfectly was Heather.

Of course, Heather did everything perfectly. She knew the words to every song there was in heaven. She could play her harp in perfect rhythm and say her prayers with just the right inflection of her voice. Her halo was the straightest in the school, and she never, ever slouched. Most of all, though, she always acted like an angel.

Heather never said a word that was unkind, and she smiled sweetly no matter what someone called her.

She gave up her place in line if she was asked, and she shared her rainbows and sunbeams with anyone who needed them.

Yes, Heather was the most perfect little angel in heaven. That's why all the other angels were shocked when Hugh gave her wings and she couldn't fly.

"What's wrong?" Heather frowned as she beat her wings hard without moving even an inch off the floor.

"Maybe they're too long," suggested Hugh, and he gave her a smaller size.

Heather tried them on. "Oh, they're much better," said Heather, "So light and comfortable." Then, flapping her feathers in earnest, she jumped off her desk and landed in a pot of heavenly ink.

The other little angels giggled quietly as Hugh helped her up and took off the wings. "Perhaps these wings are too thick," he suggested. "Here's a nice sleek set of feathers. Try them on."

Heather did. Then she ran across the school room, out the front door, and jumped off the school house steps. Unfortunately, those wings didn't work either, for Heather spun through the air, head-over-heels, and landed in a cloud puddle.

"Let's try more height," said Hugh hopefully.

He gave her a boost up to the roof of the school house. Heather flapped her wings harder and harder. With a mighty leap, she dove into the air and landed in a heap in front of all the little angels.

"It's not the wings!" Heather cried. "It's me! Something's wrong with me!"

And there certainly was a lot wrong with her at the moment. Her robe was wet and stained with ink. Her halo was bent, and her golden hair was snarled. Never in her life had Heather looked so imperfect.

Heather ran to a window in the front of the school to look at her reflection in the glass. However, she wasn't looking at her robe or her hair or her halo. She was looking deep into her own blue eyes, for she knew that flying was the greatest test of an angel's perfection.

Heather turned to watch the other little angels with their new wings, flapping and flying and diving about not-so-perfectly. "What's wrong with me?" Heather sniffed as Hugh came and gently put a hand on her shoulder. "Why can they fly, when I can't?"

Hugh looked at the other angels flying precariously around the school house. "Well, they're not perfect," agreed Hugh.

"But I am perfect," Heather argued. "I do everything right. I should fly!"

Hugh looked at her thoughtfully for a long time. Finally he said, "Look at yourself in the glass and tell me how you feel."

Heather looked at her robe and her hair. She frowned. "I feel disgusted and angry and... Oh, no!" Heather put her hand over her mouth, horrified.

"That's not the proper way to feel."

Hugh laughed. "Now look at the other little angels and tell me how you feel."

"Oh, no," Heather gasped. "I'm jealous. I can't be jealous."

"But you are," said Hugh gently. "Don't try so hard not to be. Then you'll find out why you can't fly."

So, day after day, Heather came to school and put on her wings and tried to fly. Day after day, she had to watch the other little angels rise above her, practicing their flight while she stayed on the school house steps. And, day after day, she discovered there were many things she felt inside her heart that angels shouldn't feel, like anxiousness and sadness and pride.

Then, one day, Heather took off her wings and left school early. She didn't even tell Hugh goodbye. She walked for a long time by the edge of the cloud, staring at the sky all around her and the earth below.

Finally Heather stopped beside her own cloud bed to watch the sun slip behind the edge of the earth. "If I can't fly," Heather told herself, "I'll never keep watch over a newborn baby or help rainbows stretch across the sky."

The sky began to darken. Heather's lip trembled as she stared up at the stars sparkling in the twilight. "If I can't fly, I'll never kiss a star or flutter down to earth to whisper goodness into a young child's ear."

She turned to see the moon peek out from behind the dark earth. "If I can't fly, then I'm not perfect," she said very softly. "And if I'm not a perfect angel," Heather whispered with a quiver in her throat, "I think my heart will break."

The moon rose slowly through the sky. Heather cried. The stars twinkled above her. She cried all night long. Then, as the last star faded in the sky, Heather sat up and watched it go.

"Perhaps I'm just not meant to fly," she said with a long, sad sigh. She looked to the east where a golden glow filled the sky. "But I can still be helpful," Heather decided with a definite nod.

Heather waved at a bird flying far below the cloud. "Even if I can't fly, I can sing to the birds or gather raindrops and snowflakes to sprinkle down on earth," she told herself happily.

Then, with a yawn, Heather stood up and took a step toward her cloud bed. "But first of all," she said, "I can go to sleep."

Heather climbed into her cloud bed and smiled at the rising sun. "Being imperfect isn't so bad," she whispered to the huge circle of light. "When you're not perfect, you can go to sleep whenever you want."

She laid her head against her pillow and closed her eyes, listening to the wind gently push the clouds around the sky. Then, all at once, Heather realized her bed was not beneath her. To her surprise, she was drifting through the air.

Heather laughed in disbelief, and as she laughed, she floated higher and higher and higher. Up, up she went until her bed looked like a small puff beneath her. Soon she could see all of heaven stretching out through the clouds. It was a beautiful sight, and to celebrate, she did a triple somersault in mid-air. Then slowly, very slowly, she came back down.

That day Heather came to school late. Her robe was wrinkled and her hair uncombed. All the other little angels murmured among themselves.

"What happened?" Hugh asked. "Is something wrong?"

Heather stood before the class, looking very sober. "Last night," she explained, "I realized I may never be perfect and never fly, and my heart broke."

All the class nodded sympathetically. Hugh wiped a tear from his eye.

"I cried all night long," Heather continued as she went to the closet and took out her wings and handed them back to Hugh.

"Finally I decided I could still be helpful, even if I couldn't fly or be perfect, and I felt so much better," Heather said. "I felt light, like I was floating in the air."

Then Heather smiled. It wasn't that sweet angel smile she had always used before, but a full-fledged, genuine grin. "And, all at once, I discovered I didn't

58

need wings to fly," she announced as she rose slowly up into the air.

She looked down at all the little angels and Hugh. They stared at her with open mouths and wide eyes. Then, to everyone's delight, she flew around the school room. It wasn't a perfect flight, but she didn't care, for she felt very, very good inside.

So, as Hugh watched proudly, Heather joined the other angels in their flying lessons, swooping and diving and rising high above the school house. And, as she flew, she grinned at all the little angels, wobbling around with their wings. However, she wasn't making fun of them, even though they needed wings to fly; for Heather understood, now, what it meant to be perfect.

Yes, at last, Heather understood the secret of perfection. Perfection didn't come from flying the highest or straightest. Perfection didn't mean acting angelic or looking tidy. The secret of perfection, Heather knew, was just feeling happy with yourself.

Finally, Heather perched on the high peak of the school house roof and stared across the sky at the sun shining through the clouds. Inside, she felt as peaceful and sunny as a little angel could.

Then she looked down at her wrinkled robe and her tangled hair and gave a happy nod. "Yes," she whispered to herself with satisfaction. "I am peaceful and sunny and... perfect."

The Listener

In a land, long ago, by the banks of the wide Wynn River, the great city of Hive's Heath flourished. It was a wealthy city because of the honey it produced. In fact, the city looked as busy as a hive of bees making honey in their combs, for its people were always collecting and marketing and celebrating honey.

The busiest spot in the whole city was the grand market square, and it was here that Jeremy came each day to watch the crowd of people passing by. His grandmother would push him down the wide boulevard through the city in an old peddler's cart, leaving him by the fountain while she sold clay honey pots in her market stall.

Jeremy spent those hours in the square, soaking up the sun and listening to the flow of conversations all around him. No one spoke to him, for he was an invalid who looked pale and weak and useless.

One day, while he listened to a friendly argument among two men, Jeremy noticed a woman watching him. He jumped with surprise. No one ever looked at him that way. He turned aside bashfully and then looked back, only to find she had disappeared into the crowd.

With tears in his eyes, he gazed down at his bony fingers, feeling like he had lost something wonderful. Then he saw a shadow cross his hand. He looked up to see the woman standing beside him. She was tall and dark-skinned. Her head was covered with a colorful cloth decorated by an unfamiliar pattern, like a sun with many arms of flame encircling it.

"You're not from here, are you?" Jeremy asked. "You're from far away."

The woman nodded. She sat by him on the edge of the fountain and laid her hand gently on Jeremy's, whispering in a strange accent, "You are sad. Please speak."

But Jeremy couldn't speak. He wasn't accustomed to sharing his thoughts with anyone. He looked again at his hands.

"Do not worry," said the woman softly. "I have heard you in your silence. You need not speak."

Jeremy looked at her. Her eyes shone golden in the morning light. Her face was calm and gentle and focused on him. She wasn't looking through him to someone else like other people did. All his life he'd felt invisible, but right now, this woman made him feel solid. He knew that whatever he said to her would be important and would be heard.

"No," said Jeremy suddenly. "I want to speak."

"I will listen," she said softly. "Please speak."

"It's just that no one ever talks to me," Jeremy began with a tremble in his voice. "I'm useless, you see. I have a weak heart and weak lungs. I can't do anything, so no one is interested in me. They're busy with things, busy like the bees. They have a purpose." Jeremy stopped a moment, embarrassed at talking so long.

"Yes," said the woman simply, "You feel no purpose."

Jeremy nodded.

"You would want a purpose?" the woman asked.

Jeremy sighed deeply. "If there was something I could do, that would be wonderful."

"What do you do now, each day?" the woman asked.

"Nothing," replied Jeremy.

"You were doing something when I first saw you," the woman assured him.

Jeremy thought back to the moment when he first saw the stranger. "I was listening to an argument. That's all."

"You like to listen?" The woman smiled.

"Oh, yes." Jeremy burst into a smile himself. "I make a game of listening and each time I choose what to listen to. Sometimes it's the noises of the whole city all at once. I hear everything—the carts, the horses, the people, the wind—together like a grand concert in the square. Other days, it's the little things

I listen for—a leaf blowing against the bricks in the square or the click, click, click of someone walking by or the hum of a mother to her baby sound asleep."

Jeremy took a deep breath and continued, "Some days it's names—all the people's names I can hear as they talk around me. Sometimes it's the fountain—trickling down like a gentle melody that changes the more I listen."

Jeremy stopped a moment to watch the woman's face. She looked delighted to be hearing what he said. "And sometimes," he grinned, "I even listen to things that make no noise—the marble of the fountain or the flowers growing in those boxes over there or the feelings hidden in my heart." The boy shook his head in amazement and added, "It's wonderful. You can't hear a sound, but still you can listen."

Then Jeremy fell silent and the woman squeezed his hand, nodding with understanding. "I know," she whispered. "I know. I am a listener."

"A listener?" Jeremy asked. "What is a listener?"

"Do you, in this city, have teachers and dancers and drum beaters and merchants and beekeepers and storytellers?" the woman replied.

"Yes." Jeremy nodded.

"Do you, in this city, have listeners?"

"No." Jeremy shook his head.

"A city needs its listeners, especially a city as busy as bees," she said. "In my city, I am a listener."

"What do you do?" Jeremy asked in earnest. He felt a shiver in his spine.

"Listen," she answered simply.

"To what?" Jeremy wondered.

"To noises and flowers and names," she said, "And troubles of the heart."

"Ah!" Jeremy sighed. "If only the people in this town would stop and listen. They're all too busy."

The woman smiled. "But you are not."

"No." Jeremy smiled back. "I am not."

"So now you know your purpose." She tapped his hand matter-of-factly.

Jeremy looked at her and stammered, "A listener? I can be a listener?"

"Yes," the woman said. "The children need it. Who in this town listens to the children?"

Jeremy nodded. "But how?" Jeremy wondered. "How do I do it?"

"Listen," she explained. "They will come."

Then the woman rose as if to go. Jeremy touched her robe and pleaded with his eyes for her to stay.

She took a step beyond him into the crowd, but turned back to say, "Early this spring, when I was listening to the wind in a stormy sky, I heard the sadness of a young boy far away across the mountain. I knew I must come here to find a boy named Jeremy and listen to the words he needed to say."

She smiled down at him. Jeremy looked at her

face beneath the cloth of the suns. He stared deep into her golden eyes, listening to the softness of her breath. Then he smiled. "Your name is Keesha," he told her. "I have heard it somewhere... somewhere in the wind. I didn't know what it meant."

"Yes. I am Keesha." The woman beamed like the sun. "And always will I listen. Always will I hear you. If you need me, I will come again. I will always come." Then she disappeared into the crowd completely.

Jeremy sat, trembling, listening to the pounding in his heart. He wondered if Keesha had been a dream. Then he heard the laughter of some children playing in the fountain. His trembling stopped. Remembering his purpose, he watched the children with his eyes and his ears and his heart.

Suddenly a girl was before him, sitting on the marble of the fountain, staring into the water with tears in her eyes. She looked up at Jeremy fearfully.

Jeremy smiled. He knew what to do. He touched her shoulder gently. "You look sad," Jeremy said. "Tell me. I will listen."

Dragon Soup

Far away, in a land of jungles and mountains and mist, there once lived a beautiful girl named Tonlu. She worked everyday in her father's fields of rice and beans, which were etched into the steep mountainside like a giant set of steps. The work was hard but she loved it, especially the way her whole family sang together as they planted and weeded the crops.

In the evening, when the work was done, Tonlu and her younger brothers and sisters would sit at the edge of the terraces, eating their supper and watching the people of the village far below move about like tiny ants.

"Oh, how I'd hate to live in the village," said Tonlu one evening as she ate her bean soup.

"But, sister, there would be so much more to do in the village than here," argued her brother Zan.

"Yes, but here you can look way down the valley and over the low hills almost as far as the sea," Tonlu explained. "Down there, in the village, those people only see the shadow of the mountains. I could never live there. I need to see far—very, very far."

69

Her brother was about to argue back when he spotted a tall figure climbing the steep path to their home. "It's the merchant," Zan said anxiously. "Why is he coming here?"

"Father owes him money," Tonlu said slowly. "That's why he has come."

The merchant was greeted solemnly by Tonlu's father, and the two men went inside the small house that was the family's home. All the children huddled together on the edge of the terrace, staring at the door of the house, wondering what the visitor was saying to their father.

It wasn't long before the merchant left, and Tonlu's mother called the children in to sleep. Nothing was said about the merchant, but Tonlu could see the worry in her father's face, and when he kissed her goodnight, there were tears in his eyes.

It was early morning when Zan shook Tonlu awake. "Come outside," he whispered as he pointed to the door.

Tonlu rose from her mat on the floor and pulled on her clothes. She met Zan at the edge of the ter-race. "Is something wrong?" she asked.

Zan nodded. "I heard Mother and Father talk last night," the boy explained. "Father doesn't have the money to pay the merchant, and he only has two weeks to find enough. If he can't, he must give the farm to the merchant or..." Zan paused a moment, looking gravely at his beautiful sister. "Or he must let the merchant claim you for his bride."

Tonlu sucked in her breath. "Oh, I couldn't," she cried. "Not him. Not down there in the village."

"But if you don't marry the merchant, then we'll lose the farm," Zan sighed. "We will starve."

"No we won't," Tonlu said. "We will find enough money to pay him."

"Where?" Zan asked. Then he realized his sister's plan, for she was staring at the top of the mountain as if she could see into its shroud of mist. "No!" He stomped his foot. "It would be better to marry the merchant than to meet the Cloud Dragons."

"Not for me," Tonlu said fiercely. "I would rather die than marry the merchant or have Father lose this farm. Dragons always have treasure near them, and I will steal some and pay Father's debt."

Then, before her little brother could stop her, she ran up the mountain path. "Tell Father I will be back," she called to Zan from a bend in the trail. "Tell him not to worry."

Fiercely, Tonlu turned back to face the steep mountain. She took a deep breath. "At least I will be able to see what lies beyond the mountain," she said bravely. "I will see far—very, very far." Still, Tonlu trembled as she hiked the mountain trail; for she could see that today, like almost every day, the mountaintop was covered with the clouds of the dragons.

It was almost night when Tonlu crept through the cold, dark mist of the mountain toward the mouth of a giant cave. Inside, she could see two huge dragons sitting before a crackling fire. One dragon was bright red with long scaly wings. The other dragon had no wings, but wore ropes of gleaming pearls around his blue-green neck.

Tonlu stared at the pearls. Each was the size of a large melon. In the village they would bring a fortune. "I only need one," she told herself. "Just one."

All night long, she waited patiently for the dragons to sleep. It wasn't until dawn that she saw them lay down and close their eyes. Then she crept to the mouth of the cave and tip-toed up to the blue-green dragon to touch a pearl. It felt as smooth as silk.

Pushing the pearls apart, Tonlu found the rope that held them together. Not knowing another way to get one free, she gnawed on the thick string carefully, hoping to bite through the rope and slip off a pearl before the dragon woke.

Nearly an hour passed. Then, finally, the string broke. Slipping off a pearl, she began to tie the rope back again when, all at once, the dragon moved in his sleep. Rolling over on his side, the dragon gave a loud groan; and as he did, one end of the string pulled from Tonlu's hands. Suddenly, pearls were flying all around her and the dragon was awake.

Grabbing a pearl, Tonlu turned to run, but the

dragon reached out with his sharp claws and blocked her way. "Krall, look!" the dragon called to his companion. "Dragon Soup for lunch."

Krall, the red dragon, opened one eye. "Good job, Breen. I thought I smelled something in the air last night. Time to get the fire hot."

Breen, the blue-green dragon, took his captive and put her in a cage near the wall of the cave. He restrung his pearls and tied them around his neck. "So you like stealing pearls?" he said with a cackle in his voice.

Tonlu stared at the large iron pot Krall had placed over the fire. "I only wanted one," she whispered fearfully.

"Only one?" Breen laughed. "You thought I might not miss it?"

Tonlu shook her head. She watched the dragon come toward her to drop one pearl in front of the cage. "There. One pearl." He laughed.

Then Breen placed a second pot of water over the fire. Soon each dragon was carefully adding bits of plants and fragrant spices from earthen jars to their own boiling brew.

"Dragon Soup." Krall laughed as he stirred his pot. "You'll like it, I bet, my pretty one."

Tonlu shook her head and shrunk to the back of the cage, trembling.

"You'd better like it... at least mine," warned

Breen. "You're the judge."

Tonlu stopped trembling. She stared, bewildered, at the dragons. "The judge?" she asked.

"It's a contest," explained Breen in his high, shrill voice. "You see, my brother and I have been fighting for years over who makes the best soup, so we've been waiting for a visitor to wander up the mountain and decide for us."

"And here you are," roared Krall. "Choose which soup is the best. Then we'll set you free."

"Free?" asked Tonlu. "And you won't put me in your soup?"

"Oh, heavens no!" shuddered Krall. "That would spoil the soup." Then he lowered his voice a bit and added with a gruesome wink, "Of course, you must remember I'm a very sore loser. If you don't like my soup, I might be tempted to try a new ingredient."

"That's not fair! You're cheating!" screamed Breen as he spat at Krall. Then he turned to Tonlu and whispered, "If you choose my soup, you can keep your pearl."

"I heard that!" thundered the red dragon. He shouted to Tonlu in a voice loud enough to shake the cage she crouched in, "And if you choose my soup, I will fly you around the world through the heavens. How would you like that?"

The two dragons fell silent, waiting for a reply from Tonlu. She looked fearfully at both dragons, not

74

knowing what to say. Finally she summoned up her courage and spoke. "I would love to have the pearl, Honorable Blue-green dragon," she said nervously. "And I would love to fly on your back, Honorable Red dragon," she added quickly. "However, to be a proper judge, shouldn't I taste the soup before I decide?"

Breen shook himself, surprised. "Why, of course! What a clever girl. This is a contest. We must do it right."

So, when the soup was done, Tonlu sat down before the fire with two huge bowls in front of her. She trembled as she reached for the first giant spoon and sipped from it. Then, still trembling, she sipped from the second spoon. "I'm not sure," she said after a long silence. "They're both very good."

"But surely," Breen insisted, "Mine is the best. Try it again."

"No! Try mine," Krall roared. "It is the best."

Tonlu held up her hand to quiet them as she said, "Please. Let me think." Then Tonlu paced up and down the cave looking for a solution to her problem. She knew whichever dragon lost would be very dangerous.

"I'm not out of the soup yet," she mumbled as she walked back and forth. "I must find a way for each of them to think they've won." Suddenly, Tonlu smiled. "That's right," she whispered to herself. "They both must win."

Then she grabbed a large cup from a shelf at the

back of the cave and dragged it toward the fire. Sitting before the bowls of soup, she bowed her head to the blue-green dragon and explained, "Honorable Breen, your soup is incredibly delicious." She turned to the red dragon and bowed her head. "Honorable Krall, your soup is absolutely wonderful." She paused a moment and added, "However, there is something lacking in each that can be found in the other, so I think we need to compromise."

All at once, she dipped a spoon into the first bowl of soup and poured it into the cup. Then she took a spoonful of soup from the second bowl and mixed it into the cup. She took a sip and announced triumphantly, "Mixed together, they make the most delightful soup I have ever tasted."

Both dragons stared at her, not knowing what to say. Finally, Breen cleared his throat, "But who won?" he asked somewhat bewildered.

Tonlu smiled graciously. "Both of you won."

"Both of us?" roared Krall.

"Taste it yourself," Tonlu said as she pointed to the cup.

Breen took a sip. "Why yes, it's better," he declared.

Krall took a sip. "Much better," Krall shouted.

Tonlu bowed deeply before the Cloud Dragons. "There are times," she said, "When things turn out better if you compromise."

Then Krall took Breen's pot of soup, mixed it with his own, and poured himself a huge bowl.

"How can we thank you?" Breen said gratefully as he watched his brother gobble down the soup.

"Set me free," replied Tonlu, "And let me keep your pearl."

"Certainly!" The dragon smiled. "Is that all?"

"Well, I have always wanted to see far beyond the mountain," Tonlu explained as she turned to Krall. "Perhaps you would still be willing to give me that ride on your back?"

"Clever girl," the dragon thundered as he licked his spoon happily, "It would be my honor."

Then, without a moment's hesitation, Tonlu gathered up her pearl and climbed on the red dragon's back. They took off into the evening sky, rising above the mist that clung to the mountaintop. All at once, Tonlu could see the sun setting on the sparkling sea as Krall made a big circle and headed around the mountain. On the other side was a broad, flat plain with rivers and jungles and towns.

"Can you see beyond the mountain now?" Krall roared above the wind.

"Yes," Tonlu shouted. She took a deep breath and gazed to the edge of the horizon, adding joyfully, "Yes. I can see very, very far."

The Donkey and the Fairy Rose

Once upon a time, on a cold October night, a boy and his father stopped by the side of the road at the top of a high mountain pass. They were taking their apples to market, a trip which took two days from the small farm where they lived. The hardest part of the journey, besides the steep climb up the mountain, was camping for the night in the icy air of the pass.

Even though Arthur shivered from the cold, he felt happy as he took the blankets from the apple cart and unhitched the horse. His father was whistling his lively market tune while starting the fire. The merry song always made Arthur smile.

"Where shall I tie the horse?" Arthur asked as he led the mare away from the cart.

"That tree behind me will do," his father replied.

Then a sudden wind blasted down from the mountain peak. It whipped the flames of the fire high, scaring the horse, who reared and bolted away from Arthur down the road.

In an instant, Arthur's father was after her. "Stay with the cart," he yelled to Arthur as he slipped into the shadows of the dark road and disappeared.

Reluctantly, Arthur waited beside the fire, his heart pounding with fear. He looked around nervously, searching the night for a sign of his father. Then he caught sight of a light on the mountainside. It looked like firelight streaming through a small window.

As the full moon rose over the mountain, Arthur saw the dim outline of a house among the trees where the light shined. "I didn't know someone lived in the pass," Arthur told himself. "I must tell father."

Then, using his discovery as an excuse to leave the fire, Arthur walked a few yards down the road. The light of the moon helped him see ahead, but he couldn't make out any shadows that looked like his father.

"Perhaps he's around that bend," Arthur said hopefully to himself. However, when the boy stepped around the curve in the road, he saw no one leading a horse his way. Instead, he saw his father lying very still on the ground with his head against a large rock at the side of the road.

Arthur rushed to his side and shook him gently, calling, "Father. Father." However, his father didn't answer or stir, and his body was too heavy to lift, so Arthur ran for help toward the lighted window beside the pass.

Before long, Arthur stood before the oak door of a small stone cottage. He knocked loudly and yelled,

"Please, you've got to help me. My father's hurt."

Arthur heard a chair scrape across the floor. Then the doorknob turned. A blast of warmth hit his face as the door creaked open.

"My, my. It's a human boy," a soft voice said. "Come in."

Arthur stepped into the fire lit room and stared at a tiny round woman floating in the air before him. She had puffy red cheeks and a wide smile. A pair of delicate wings graced her back.

"You're a fairy!" he sputtered. "A real fairy!"

"My name is Merry." She nodded. "Sit down."

Arthur shook his head, remembering his father. "Oh, please," pleaded Arthur. "Please come."

But Merry had already closed the cottage door. "Now tell me what happened," she said calmly.

"We were camped by the road and our horse bolted," explained Arthur. "My father fell and hit his head. He won't wake up and the horse is gone. I can't get him home."

The little woman turned to her fire and poured some herbs into a black pot. "Then I must finish this." She nodded. "We will need it."

Arthur looked at the thick, bubbling brew. "Is it magic?" he asked. "Is it for my father?"

The fairy didn't answer. She tasted a sip of the broth. "It's perfect," she said as she licked her lips.

She hung the ladle on its hook over the hearth

and gazed thoughtfully at the fire. "Now your father. Let's see.... I can help your father," Merry said as she turned toward the boy. "But you must help too. I warn you, however, it will be difficult."

"I'll do anything," said Arthur.

"Very well, then. Go up the mountain and fetch my donkey," said Merry. "We will need the donkey."

"Certainly," said the boy. "Is that all?"

"No. On the mountain is a rose bush. It's not an ordinary rose, mind you, but a fairy rose. Pick me one and bring it here."

"I will," said Arthur.

Merry drifted over to the boy and put a hand on his shoulder. "And last," she said, "You must smile."

"Smile?" asked Arthur.

"Yes," answered Merry. "You see, there's only one way to bring that donkey down from the mountain and only one way to tame the magic rose—"

"And what is that?" Arthur interrupted eagerly.

"Now, that's a secret," Merry said with a wink, "And I'm bound by magic never to tell or it will break the spell on them. But you look like a clever boy who can figure it out with this little hint: To learn the secret of the donkey and the rose, you must act like a fairy—that means to keep a happy thought, no matter what, and smile."

Arthur shook his head. "My father's hurt. How can I smile?"

Merry leaned closer. "Do you want to help him?"

"I do!" said Arthur with tears flooding his eyes.

"Then you mustn't worry," said Merry. "That will only make you lose heart, and you'll never get the donkey or the rose."

Arthur dried his tears and took a deep breath. His face felt stiff, and his muscles twitched as he forced the corners of his mouth up. It didn't feel like a genuine smile.

"That's a beginning," said the fairy as she opened the door. "Quick, now, up the mountain. I will see to your father."

The mountain wind whipped around Arthur as he stepped from the little cottage. The boy's cheeks stung from the icy cold. His mouth quivered, wanting to let go of the smile. He looked toward the road, thinking he should forget about the fairy and her donkey and the rose. He wanted to be with his father.

Then he turned to face the mountain. "Stop worrying," he reminded himself. "Keep smiling." Bravely, he stepped forward toward the trail.

However, as Arthur climbed the steep slope, he found his courage failing. There were giant shadows everywhere, created by the full moon. They loomed around him like dark beasts. Trees scraped against each other in the wind. Arthur pinched himself. "Keep smiling," he repeated.

Suddenly, he heard something crash through the

83

bushes behind him. It let out a terrible noise like a giant rusty hinge. Arthur froze and his eyes grew wide. He heard the noise again.

"Hee haw! Hee haw!"

Then he turned to see Merry's fat little donkey standing beside a tiny brook. Arthur sighed with relief as he patted the donkey's head. He picked up the animal's rope and gave a tug. "Let's go," he said.

"Hee haw!" the donkey brayed. He wouldn't budge.

Arthur walked behind the donkey and gave a mighty push. Then, with one sharp kick from the donkey, Arthur landed on the muddy bank with a splat.

He sat in the mud, muttering angrily at the donkey, until he realized he had lost his smile. Quickly, he stretched a grin across his face, but it was too late. When he looked up, the donkey was gone. With a sigh, Arthur headed for the rose.

At the top of the mountain grew the fairy rose. Arthur could see it from below as he climbed the rocky trail. It glowed in the moonlight, silver and red. It was beautiful and Arthur smiled.

"This looks easy," Arthur thought as he reached the mountain peak. Before him, the flowers shimmered in the darkness, swaying in the wind. He reached out to grab one but caught a thorn. "Ow!" Arthur yelled but it sounded like "Ah!" through his smile.

Arthur giggled and tried once more, but the rose dodged sideways. "So it's a game, is it?" Arthur said to the roses.

He grabbed again and again for a magic rose, but always missed. Finally he shook his head at the rose bush in dismay. "You really are a magic rose," he said, "And stubborn, too, like that little donkey."

Arthur slumped to the ground, miserably. His cheeks ached from the cold. His fingers were full of thorns. His smile was gone, and he felt like giving up. Then he shook his head. "I'm just thinking of myself. What about Father?"

He thought of his father lying beside the road. The thought only made him feel worse. "What should I do?" he moaned.

Desperately, he searched for an answer, but all he could think of was Merry telling him to be happy and smile. So he strained hard to put the smile back where it belonged. Finally he managed it. It was a little smile, cold and stiff, but it was a start. It gave him a feeling of hope.

Then, suddenly, he remembered hitching their old horse to the cart full of apples that morning. It had been such a fine morning in their little valley as they set out for the market city to sell their crop. His father whistled the market tune all the way up the steep road toward the mountain pass.

Arthur thought of that tune now as he saw his father's happy face, so clear and strong, in his memory. It made him smile, really smile. And the smile took over. It grew and grew and grew. Soon he felt as bright as the moon glowing in the sky.

"This is how a fairy must feel," sighed Arthur.

He grinned at a blossom and sang his happy song until he noticed the rose had become still. It drooped a little as if asleep.

All at once, Arthur bubbled with excitement. He reached toward the rose and plucked it from its prickly stem. "So that's the secret," he cried, "Just sing a rose to sleep."

Waving the rose triumphantly, Arthur danced around the magic bush. He jumped and clapped and shouted and turned in dizzy circles. However, when he stopped to catch his breath, he felt a tug on the magic flower. The next thing he knew, the rose was gone. Something had pulled it from his hand.

Turning, he saw the fat little donkey happily chewing the last of the petals in his mouth. "You beast!" he screamed. He stomped the ground and boxed the donkey between the ears. The donkey just brayed as if laughing at him.

And then, through his anger, Arthur remembered Merry's words. "Act like a fairy," he told himself. "Keep a happy thought, no matter what, and smile."

So Arthur hummed his father's tune to calm himself down. Then he managed a grin as he spoke to the donkey. "I know how to tame the rose," Arthur said, "Now I must learn your secret."

Arthur stretched his smile from ear to ear, propping it up with his fingers just to make sure. He hummed louder and cleared his mind. In an instant, a wonderful idea came to him. He knew, now, how to get that donkey to budge.

So Arthur sat beside the bush and sang another rose to sleep. He plucked it quickly and turned back to the donkey.

"Come on fellow," he coaxed. "Here's a rose for you."

As the donkey stepped forward to eat the flower, Arthur stepped back. The donkey stepped forward again, and Arthur stepped back, too. All the way down the mountain that stubborn donkey followed the boy and the fairy rose.

The fairy was waiting at the door. "You've done well," she said.

"How can you tell?" asked Arthur.

Merry put her hand on the boy's bony shoulder. "I can tell by the look of you," she said softly. "Now sit down."

"Sit down?" asked Arthur.

The fairy pointed to the black pot over the fire. "For the stew."

"That's stew?" said Arthur in dismay. "I thought that was magic to heal my father."

Merry shook her head. "I never told you it was magic."

87

"But my father," Arthur protested.

Merry looked at him patiently. "Your father's already had his stew."

"His stew? He's already had his stew?" Arthur asked in disbelief. "You mean he's all right?"

"When I found your father, he was awake. So, with the help of a little fairy magic, I got him back to the cottage," Merry explained. "A good thought from you and a bowl of my stew have done him wonders. He's just gone out to find the horse."

"But the donkey? The rose?" Arthur stammered.

"I had my reasons. You'll see," winked Merry.

Just then, there was a knock at the door. Arthur opened it to find his father staring at him.

"Father!" Arthur shouted. He hugged him hard.

Arthur's father hugged him back. Then he shook his head with a sigh. "The horse is gone, Son. I don't know how we'll get the apples to market now."

Arthur glanced over at the little wooden table where a bowl of steaming stew waited to be eaten. Beside it lay the fairy rose he had picked. Arthur winked at Merry.

"I know how, Father," Arthur said. "I know exactly how."

Next morning, the crisp air rang with a merry whistle as an apple cart creaked slowly over the mountain pass. The whistler was Arthur's father, and pulling the cart, was the stubborn donkey.

Out in front, leading the way, was Arthur holding a beautiful red rose just beyond the donkey's reach.

And, of course, spread across Arthur's happy face was a smile.

The Toys of Sharing

A long time ago, when there were kings and queens and magic, four children hiked through a steep mountain pass toward the ruins of a castle. Kammer, the tallest, led the way. He was followed by his sister, Ruta, and his cousins, Bessay and Lons.

As they hiked along, they argued about whether they were walking too fast or too slow or too far without a rest. Finally, when they reached the castle, they were so grumpy that the dark window slits and silent stone walls looming high above their heads didn't bother them a bit.

Without waiting for the others, Kammer stomped angrily across the empty drawbridge. He lit the torch from his pack and stormed into the darkness of the castle. The other children ran to catch up. Soon they were stumbling along crumbling corridors, climbing rickety flights of stairs, passing through room after room and arguing endlessly.

"I bet there's no treasure here," Kammer grumbled as they walked among the echoes of the grand dinner hall. "Father says there's nothing left of the High

Wizard's riches now. They were stolen years ago after he died and left no heirs to claim his kingdom."

"Your father's wrong," Lons growled, reaching for the torch. "There's treasure here like the stories say. We're just not looking in the right places. Let me lead."

"And where would you look?" Kammer snorted, swinging the torch away from his cousin. "Do you have a map to show the way?"

Lons scowled and fell silent, but then Ruta started up. "I think there could be something here... something that was overlooked. But if you don't believe in those old stories, Kammer, why should we follow you? Let me lead."

Kammer shook his head. "I'm the oldest and the strongest. I lead."

Just then, little Bessay, who had her head cocked toward the front of the hall, sighed. "You're all a bunch of squawking chickens," she scolded. "Please, be quiet and let me listen."

"Listen?" asked Lons.

"Yes," Bessay answered. "Can't you hear it?"

Kammer stopped in the middle of the dark, cold room. "What? Hear what?"

"Hush!" Bessay whispered. "Hush!"

"I don't hear anything," Lons grumbled.

"Please," groaned Bessay. "Please, just be quiet."

So the other children paused a moment in their

argument to let Bessay listen. However, as their anger faded into silence, so did their courage. Ruta shivered in the stillness. Lons looked nervously around him. Kammer raised the torch even higher to illuminate the shadows. Then Bessay strained her ears to sift through all the muffled echoes she could hear within the room.

Somewhere water dripped from the ceiling, and an animal scuttled across the floor. A bird in the chimney blended its wing beats into the echoes of the hall. Even their quiet breathing resounded in the empty chamber like an endless droning chant. However, something else was mixed into the gentle rumble of the echoes, and Bessay wanted to find out what it was.

"It's over there," Bessay said as she pointed through the blackness. She took a few steps but turned around. "No," she said. "It's over there."

"I don't hear it," Lons insisted.

"Listen. It's like... well, like music." Bessay explained. Then her eyes grew wide. "Yes!" she shouted. "It's music!"

"Yes... yes... yes.... It's music... music... music," rang her echo as Kammer and Ruta and Lons huddled together, cringing at the strength of their cousin's voice in the darkness.

Finally, though, the echo settled and Bessay hurried forward, listening keenly with her ears. She wandered through the shadows, turning this way and that. Finally, she came back to face her cousins. "It must be the echoes," she said with disappointment. "I can't find out where it's coming from."

Kammer waved his torch importantly. "Follow me!" he said. "I'll find it."

Ruta put out her arm to stop him. "Wait!" she said with alarm. "If it's music, someone must be playing it."

Everyone stopped breathing for a second. Then Lons whispered anxiously, "Ghosts! There's ghosts here."

"Or robbers," added Ruta. "Or—"

"Or something wonderful," Bessay interrupted as she listened carefully. "Can't you hear it? It's beautiful and it's magic."

"Magic can be good, but it can be bad," Kammer cautioned.

Bessay shook her head. "If you just listen, then you'll know it's something good."

So, at last, with much prodding from Bessay, the other children settled down to listen. At first, only Ruta caught the gentle melody, but as she did the notes grew stronger. Then Kammer began to hear it. Bessay nodded happily.

"Yes," she said. "It's getting louder. The more we concentrate, the stronger it gets."

Suddenly, Lons grabbed Bessay's hand. "I hear it," he whispered. And just as he said that, the melody broke through the echoes, clearly, as if it were right beside them.

"It's a flute," Bessay whispered joyfully. "Oh, it's lovely. It makes me want to dance."

"But where is it?" grunted Kammer as he looked around.

"What about there?" Ruta said, pointing through the darkness.

"Yes, there," agreed Bessay as they all spotted a faint glow where a tiny alcove joined the room.

"Ghosts," Lons stuttered as he stared at the light.

"Not ghosts," whispered Bessay. "Magic." She stepped forward into the shadows, calling, "Follow me."

However, the others didn't budge. They stood, terrified, until they heard Bessay shout, "Oh, come! Come quick! Oh, look! It's beautiful!" Then their curiosity overcame their fear, and all three stumbled through the darkness toward Bessay and the light.

"It's beautiful," Bessay repeated as they came near.

"Is it the flute?" asked Ruta breathlessly.

"Yes," said Bessay. "But look!"

Ruta stepped into the alcove beside Bessay. She looked down at something small and square and bright on the floor. "It's a box!" she cried.

"A crystal box!" Lons stammered as he peered over his cousin's shoulder.

"A box of toys!" Kammer whispered in awe.

Kammer set the torch in a holder by the door,

then all the children stood silently, watching the four magical toys that could be seen inside. The first was the little flute. It was golden, and its keys moved all by themselves as it played its cheery tune. Bessay looked at it in wonder and sighed.

The second was a tiny winged horse, which flew around the box in circles. As Ruta watched him, he looked at her and winked.

The third toy was a top with silver edges, twirling endlessly on its axis. It was very small, but Kammer could swear that, as he watched it, it grew and grew and grew in size.

Last was a book, a miniature book, with magic moving pages that turned mysteriously for Lons to read.

Lons reached toward the magic box. "Let's open it."

"How?" asked Kammer, looking for a latch or keyhole somewhere on the top.

"There's no way," Ruta agreed.

Kammer felt the delicate crystal for any sign of a hinge or a lid. "We could break it open," he suggested.

"No," said Bessay suddenly. "Something's written there on the side of the box."

Kammer looked to the spot in the clear crystal where Bessay pointed. "There's nothing there," he said.

"It's faint, I know, but look harder," Bessay insisted.

"Oh, yes," said Kammer slowly. "I see something."

"What does it say?" Ruta asked as she poked her head between her brother's and her cousin's for a look.

"I don't know," Bessay answered. "I can't quite read it."

"Let me try," said Lons, pushing his way in between the others. He stared hard at the box, but the writing wasn't clear enough to be understood.

"Stop shoving!" growled Kammer as Lons pushed even closer.

"I'm not shoving!" argued Lons.

"You're shoving me!" yelled Ruta, falling backwards with a frown.

"Hush!" warned Bessay. She pointed toward the light. "It's getting dimmer."

All the children watched in dismay as the soft light flickered and went out. The children could see the box in the torchlight, but not the toys inside. Even the melody of the little flute was hard to hear. It blended with the echoes of the larger room behind them, once again.

"What happened?" groaned Kammer, thinking of that spinning top he could no longer see.

"The horse! He's gone!" cried Ruta with tears in her eyes.

"So's the book," sniffed Lons.

"Nothing's gone," reminded Bessay. "The toys and

97

the magic are still here. The only thing that's gone is our cooperation. We're fighting again."

Bessay's cousins looked at her with disbelief. "So what?" Kammer scoffed.

"We won't open the box unless we work together, that's what," Bessay explained. "We couldn't hear the flute back in the hall, either, until we stopped fighting long enough to listen."

"How do you know all this?" Ruta asked suspiciously.

"I don't, really," Bessay said, "But I remember a story from a peddler, years ago, when I was just three. It was something about a crystal box and inside were the Toys of Sharing."

Kammer scratched his forehead. "Toys of Sharing? I never heard that story."

"Nor I," said Ruta.

"Nor I," said Lons.

"I've never heard it since," said Bessay, "And I don't remember much of it at all, but I've always imagined finding a box like this someday."

Lons looked at the box puzzled. "Why hasn't someone stolen it long ago?" he wondered.

"Perhaps," Ruta offered, "No one could see the box in the darkness."

"Yes, that's how the story went," agreed Bessay. "If someone was angry or frightened or alone, the box would never be found here in the darkness. These are

98

Toys of Sharing. They must be shared with someone, not fought over or stolen away."

All the children were quiet for a moment as they watched the box, hoping the magic would come back.

"Let's listen," suggested Lons.

"Yes," agreed Ruta. "We'll listen all together."

"Be very quiet," whispered Kammer.

Bessay just smiled and nodded and cocked her head to listen. Her cousins joined her. Soon the little flute could be heard, again, cheerfully playing a tune. The soft light began to grow once more until they could all see the tiny toys that waited within.

"Now we'll read the words together," Bessay said as she leaned down toward the writing on the box.

"But I can't make it out. It's too faint." Ruta frowned.

"No, it's not," Kammer whispered. "See. It's clearer."

"Ah, yes," said Lons. "It's getting deeper and clearer and... there it is."

Suddenly, they saw each word etched into the crystal stone as if it had always been that way. The writing was in the old style—from the days of the high wizard.

"Read together," Bessay whispered. Then they read aloud the writing on the box. It said, "Join hand to hand and heart to heart to touch the Toys of Sharing."

"Is that all?" Kammer asked.

"That's enough," answered Bessay as she grabbed his hand.

Ruta grabbed Kammer's other hand, and then Lons joined in to make a complete circle around the box.

"Should we close our eyes?" Lons asked.

"Yes," said Bessay. "Let's."

And so they closed their eyes, waiting for something grand to happen. The little flute played louder. A shiver went through Bessay.

"Heart to heart," Bessay whispered.

"And no peeking," Ruta giggled.

"But when will we know to look?" asked Kammer.

"We'll know," Lons assured him. "We'll know."

It wasn't long before their fingers tingled with magic and their hearts felt open and full. Kammer wondered how he could ever have been angry with the others, just as Ruta forgave her brother for every fight they ever had. Lons smiled with a deep joy as he thought of his cousins. Little Bessay stood in perfect stillness, feeling as if she glowed.

It could have been hours that they stood there or only minutes; but when the children opened their eyes, they saw the lid of the box raise magically, allowing them to reach inside. Bessay knelt down and pulled out the little top, handing it to Kammer. "You're the oldest," she smiled. "You be first."

Kammer grinned and set the top down on the floor. It spun faster and faster and faster; and as it spun, it grew. The children's eyes widened with surprise as the top began to shimmer. Instantly, it was almost as tall as the tiny room.

Kammer watched the top spin around the little room. Then it slowed enough for him to notice some silver handles fastened to the top's outer edge. "Come on!" Kammer shouted. "Let's go for a spin."

He reached up and grabbed a handle. The others grabbed one too. Soon they were all laughing and shouting and spinning wildly around the alcove.

In the end it was Kammer who shouted, "Enough!" He dropped from the giant top and fell on the floor—dizzy, but happy. The others followed him to the ground. Suddenly they were all staring, once again, at a very tiny top wobbling in the center of the room.

The top came to a halt at Kammer's feet. He picked it up and set it inside the crystal box. Then he reached for the flute and gave it to Bessay. Bessay stared in wonder as the little instrument played its happy tune. Then she sat it on the floor in front of her and began to dance.

Bessay twirled and stepped and jumped and turned to the cheerful tune, which grew livelier by the moment. As she danced, she motioned with her hands for her cousins to join her. "Come on!" she urged. "Dance with me."

Ruta stood up and turned on her toes, but Kammer and Lons held back boyishly. Then Bessay surprised them by leaping clear across the room and landing halfway up the wall. She danced to the ceiling and stood there twirling upside-down. Soon all the cousins were leaping around the room as if they were wild goats on the mountain top.

Finally Bessay stopped before the little flute. She whispered softly, "Enough." Its music hushed; and Lons, who was still dancing up the wall, fell to the floor with a thud.

"Ouch!" Lons said with a laugh.

"I'm sorry," giggled Bessay as she helped him up. Then she picked up the little flute and laid it gently back into the box where it belonged.

"What shall we do next?" Bessay asked as she stared at the horse and the book. She started to reach for the horse, but with a quick smile at Lons, she picked up the book. "I think we need a rest," she said. "A story would be nice."

Lons trembled as he settled down to watch the pages of the tiny book turn slowly in front of him. The pictures flowed magically from page to page as if a miniature world was caught inside the flat surface of the paper. Lons began reading out loud about a forest at the edge of the sea. Then his eyes grew wide as he stared at the page in front of him. "Look!" he shouted. "It's me!"

The others gathered around to see their own pictures in the little book. And then, all at once, they were part of the book itself, climbing across the pages as the scenery shifted magically and the words moved all around them.

"Oh!" shouted Lons. "This is incredible!"

Soon the children found themselves hoisting the sails of a ship as Lons read on about the sights that lay ahead. They sailed far from shore past whales and sharks and flying fish. They swam through reefs of coral and sunken shipwrecks full of treasure. They made friends with mermaids and dolphins, and even a baby octopus came out from its cave to play.

It wasn't until they saw the giant tentacles of the baby's mother reaching from the cave, that Lons read out, "Enough." Suddenly, they were all sprawled across the alcove, once again, with the unmistakable taste of salt on their lips.

"That wasn't much of a rest." Lons laughed as he put the book back in the box. Then he held out his hand, and the little flying horse landed on his palm. He walked to Ruta, grinning. "Perhaps the best will be last."

Ruta looked at the horse wistfully. The steed winked at her and spread his wings to fly. A wind sprang up all around them. All at once, they were high in the air, circling through the clouds, riding on the horse's back. Far below them was the valley and their homes.

"Oh, look!" Ruta cried, clinging to the horse's

mane. "It's Mama and Papa."

"There's our village," shouted Lons. "And the river."

"And there's my garden," called Bessay, "And my favorite apple tree."

"Lons, look! There's the stone fort we always fight over," cried Kammer. Then he added sheepishly, "From up here, it doesn't look like anything to fight over, does it?"

"No, Cousin, it doesn't," laughed Lons.

Bessay looked all around her from horizon to horizon. There was an endless line of mountains behind mountains with valleys tucked in between. Lakes flashed brightly in the sun; and far, far away was the great curve of ocean water called the Mystic Sea.

"Just look how huge the world is from up here," Bessay said. "There's so much world to share. You'd think it would be easy for us to get along."

Kammer grinned. "Maybe it will be from now on. Don't you think so Ruta?"

However, Ruta didn't answer. Anxiously, she watched the shadows lengthening across the forests and the towns. Soon the sun would set, and they would be called in to supper, but she didn't want the ride to end.

Finally, Kammer whispered into her ear, "It's getting dark."

Ruta nodded. She sighed and took a very deep

breath. Then she said, rather reluctantly, "Enough."

The winged horse circled slowly downward and settled in the trees behind Ruta's cottage. Kammer and Bessay and Lons slipped off the back of the great steed. They looked up at Ruta.

"Come on," said Kammer. "Supper's waiting."

Ruta hugged the horse's neck and sighed. "I want to keep him."

Bessay looked at her cousin. "Do you think he's yours to keep?"

Ruta frowned. "But we did find the toys. Don't they belong to us?"

"I don't think they belong to anyone," Bessay answered. "They are toys to be shared, not kept."

Ruta scowled. "But what if someone else finds them?"

Kammer rested his hand on Ruta's shoulder. "If someone else finds the toys, they'll learn to use them wisely and put them back again."

"Yes," Lons said quietly. "And when we climb the mountains again, someday, the crystal box will be waiting for us."

With another reluctant sigh, Ruta slid off the horse as he spread his wings to fly. Up he soared, higher and higher, until he only looked like a tiny toy horse in the sky. Then he disappeared over the mountains in the direction of the ancient castle.

Ruta watched the sky for a long while, hoping to

get one more glimpse of the flying horse. Finally she turned to the others. "Let's go back soon," she said earnestly, "As soon as we can."

The boys nodded silently, while Bessay smiled and took her cousin's hand. "Yes," she said, simply. "Let's."

The First Giving

There was once a time in the ancient land of Gafha when each family was a member of a clan. These clans fought against each other because of hatreds passed down from parents to children to grandchildren to great-grandchildren. Some clans had been bitter enemies for centuries, like the Clan of the Windfire and the Clan of the Mountain Rain.

In the small village of Tiku lived a boy named Ursi, who belonged to the Clan of the Mountain Rain. Ursi was twelve, and he spent each day running the mountain trails through the forest instead of hunting or herding the goats. Only Ursi was permitted to do this, for he had won the honor of running for his clan in the Challenge.

The Challenge was a race, and every year each clan sent one twelve-year-old to the great city of Hiyu to compete in it. Ursi was determined to win the race for his clan, so he trained hard each day, running faster and faster and faster. As he ran, he kept his mind filled with rage and hate; for that, he was told, was the secret to winning the race.

109

One day Ursi took a trail he had never seen before. It led beyond the forest to a split in a rocky cliff that, at first, looked very shallow. Yet, when Ursi peered into its shadow, he could tell it was deep.

"Hello," said a voice from the darkness.

Ursi jumped. It was a girl's voice.

"Come in," she said in a tone, soft and peaceful and truly inviting.

Ursi looked up at the hot sun. It pulsed like the rhythm of his heart when he was running. A bead of sweat dripped off his forehead as he stepped to the cool of the shade between the stone. He looked around him, blinded by the sudden darkness.

"Who are you?" he asked, seeing only shadows.

"My name is Seffalie," she answered.

"My name is Ursi," he replied.

There was silence for a moment. Then the sun spots cleared from Ursi's eyes. He could see her outline, now, and something shimmering on her hand. Ursi wondered what it could be that gleamed even in the darkness. Then he knew. He put his hand to the dagger at his side.

"You wear the Stone of the Windfire," he challenged her. "You are my enemy."

"Yes, I am of the Windfire people, but I am not an enemy," she answered.

Ursi glanced behind him. "Is this a trap?" he asked. "Have you brought me here to die?"

110

"No," she said. "I have called you to freedom."

"Freedom," Ursi scoffed. "I need no freedom."

She didn't answer. She only took his hand and led him deeper into the rock.

They walked in darkness. The path was smooth underfoot and Seffalie clearly knew the way. Ursi kept alert for danger, but still followed. There was something compelling in the gentle touch of this Windfire girl.

Finally, she paused and said, "I have waited a year for someone to come." She pushed open a door, and Ursi's eyes were flooded with light once again.

Ursi shaded his eyes from the glare. Slowly, he focused on the face of the enemy girl. He saw the black hair and dark skin of the Windfire Clan, but when his eyes adjusted to the light, he was astounded at the beauty he saw before him.

She had the high cheeks, the elegant nose and the dark, flashing eyes like all Windfire people; but it wasn't those that made Ursi's heart flutter. Her face was different. It lacked the harshness that Ursi had always seen, not just from the Windfire people, but from his own. She had that peaceful quality which could only be seen on the face of a baby as it slept. It made Seffalie seem absolutely radiant.

Seffalie swept her hand through the air gracefully. "Look," she said. "This is the gift that I must give you."

Ursi gazed around him. He saw a room of rock and another door. There was a table, a chair and a simple bed. Above them, a shaft of sunlight filtered through a rough opening in the ceiling.

"This is the waiting place," she explained. "This is where I have waited for you this past year."

Ursi looked at her bewildered. "You've lived here all alone? What about your people?"

"I have no people, now," she said. "They would kill me if they found me."

"Why? Did you betray them?"

Seffalie sat down on a rock ledge near the shaft of sunlight. She looked up at the small patch of blue sky showing through the opening. "Two years ago I found this place. There was someone waiting for me— someone from the Clan of the Ice Clouds."

"The Ice Clouds?" Ursi protested. "Their land is on the other side of Hiyu. How could they get here?"

"This is a mysterious place. I came here by walking on the desert plain of the Windfire Clan," explained Seffalie. "I think there is a path for every- one who must find their way here."

Ursi shook his head, remembering the trail had led through the forest. He couldn't believe Seffalie.

Seffalie smiled. "Just listen," she said. "You won't understand, not yet."

Then she went on to tell her story. "Her name was Diha, and she told me her story as I tell you. I

112

didn't understand, and I left to return to my people, but her beauty haunted me. She looked as peaceful as a newborn child and I longed to see her face again."

Ursi stood, absorbed by the sound of her voice; and as he listened, it almost seemed the words told a story that was his own.

"And then," Seffalie continued, "Just last year, after the Celebration of the Flames, we were raided. My father was killed. I watched from behind a rock as the warriors swept over our village. They took all we had and vanished. Then, as my mother and brothers and sisters crept back to help the wounded, I heard a noise from the gully to the west of me. I knew some-one was hurt, so I went to find them, but when I got there the wounded man was the enemy. I recognized him as the one who'd killed my father."

"Did you take revenge?" asked Ursi breathlessly.

Seffalie shook her head. "I hid him in a sand cave and bound his wounds. Every day I brought him water and food."

"Why?" asked Ursi in disbelief.

Seffalie stood. She took his hand and led him to the other doorway. "Because of this," she said as she pointed to the arch above the door, "And the memory of the girl called Diha."

Ursi stared at the archway. There were words etched into the stone. He stood back, reading slowly, "The first giving is the hardest, but the most blessed with joy." He shook his head. "I don't understand."

"You won't," Seffalie said quietly. "Not yet."

Ursi stared at the words and read them again and again. They made no sense to him. Still, something quivered in his heart each time he said them.

"What happened to your enemy?" Ursi asked.

"I came one day and he was gone." Seffalie said simply. "But Saru, my sister, followed me that day. She found the blood soaked rags and the water flask and the broken dagger he left behind. My people do not carry daggers, and so she knew of my treachery."

"My clan carries daggers," Ursi said.

"I know." Seffalie nodded. "He was of the Mountain Rain."

Ursi stared, transfixed, at Seffalie. A long time passed in silence. She watched him calmly—her face radiant as ever. And then, without knowing it, Ursi reached out and stroked her cheek. It was a gesture of affection among his people.

All at once, Ursi caught himself and withdrew. "I'm sorry," he mumbled awkwardly. He stared at the ground in shame, but deep inside he felt his heart quiver again.

"Saru challenged me on the spot," Seffalie explained. "So I turned and walked away from my home and my family. Still, there was something soaring in my heart, for I knew I was on the trail back to this place and that girl from the Ice Cloud Clan."

"Was she here when you came?" Ursi asked.

"No," Seffalie replied softly, "But she is waiting beyond this archway. Every night, as I sleep, someone brings me food and drink. I can't help but feel it is Diha."

"But where does she live? Didn't she tell you?"

"No." Seffalie smiled. "It doesn't matter. Perhaps it is a house or a city or a whole new land. I do not know. I only know it is a place that is peaceful."

"Peaceful..." Ursi sighed. "It is hard to think of a place that is peaceful."

"It may seem so now, but you will return here someday. And then," Seffalie touched him on the arm, "And then you will understand."

Seffalie reached up and stroked his cheek gently, staring into Ursi's eyes. Then she pulled the handle of the door and stepped beneath the archway, slipping into the darkness beyond.

The door slammed shut with a solemn clank. Ursi pulled the handle. It wouldn't budge, and suddenly, Ursi felt a pain in his heart he'd never felt before.

"Seffalie!" Ursi cried out as he stared at the closed door before him. "Seffalie!"

He pounded on the door for a long time, but no one came. Finally, he glanced at the writing on the archway once more. Then he stumbled back through the cave to the brightness of the day. He stared up at that hot sun through eyes brimming with tears.

"Seffalie," he whispered as he began to run. "Seffalie."

He headed down the path, back toward Tiku. The forest closed around him. Its shadow cooled him, so he ran faster. He pushed his muscles hard; but instead of running with hate in his heart, he ran with a great sadness and the sadness wouldn't go away. Even as he lay down to sleep late that night, he watched the stars and thought of Seffalie.

It took six weeks of running over the mountain trails for Ursi to numb that sadness so he could take the Oath of the Challenge. He had practiced it many times, alone in the woods, only to burst into tears. Finally, when he could say it calmly, he went to his father and pledged to make his clan proud.

"You don't sound very hateful," his father said when Ursi was done.

"I'm just tired, Father," Ursi mumbled. "I ran very hard today."

"You do work hard," his father agreed, "But remember your oath and hate your enemies. Then you will win."

Ursi nodded wearily. He looked out through the trees. All he could think of was the peaceful face of Seffalie.

Then, on the day he was to leave for the city of Hiyu, he rose before the sun and ran up the mountain slope, trying to remember the way he had gone that

116

day when he met Seffalie.

Ursi had never found the trail back to the cliff, though he looked for it every day. However, something in him made him try once more, before he left for the race.

He stretched his legs and filled his lungs and let his body go with the rhythm of running. His mind wandered back to the memory of Seffalie. He saw her face, so peaceful and radiant, and then he heard her voice whispering as if it floated through the forest in front of him.

"The first giving is the hardest, but the most blessed with joy," he heard her say. "The first giving is the choice of freedom."

Ursi stopped, gulping in his breath, looking around him wildly for the trail to the cliff. It wasn't there. It never was there, but he felt her so close, waiting for him somewhere.

Ursi spent every minute he could searching the shadows of the forest for Seffalie. Finally, with an aching heart, he returned to his village and said goodbye to his family. Only his father would come with him to Hiyu for the journey was very dangerous.

By nightfall, they reached the great city and were met by the Guards of the Gate. Ursi's father showed them the scroll of his clan that gave them entrance to the Challenge. Then the guard made arrangements for a guide to lead them through the city to lodging near

117

the race.

Ursi didn't sleep well that night, but his mind wasn't on the Challenge. He would wake up in a sweat from dreams of running on the mountain, searching for that trail back to the cliff. And then he'd remember Seffalie's voice talking of the first giving. He knew those words were the way back to Seffalie, but what did they mean? He couldn't understand.

At last, the sun rose. It was the day of the Challenge. Ursi readied himself, listening to his father's words of advice. Then he made his way to the banners above the starting line. He took his place and looked beside him. He was surprised to see a girl there. She was tall and dark, and she stood beneath the banner of the Windfire Clan.

It wasn't often that a girl was sent to the Challenge, but Ursi knew sometimes it was done. Still, this girl unsettled him, for she looked at him with eyes of hate. He couldn't help but flinch.

"I will win," she spat at him.

Ursi didn't answer. He turned away and listened to the drums beating in preparation. He heard the call to the runners. He crouched low, and then the Challenge horn blasted through the morning. It was the signal to run.

Ursi leapt from his position and stretched his legs in exhilaration. It felt good to run the Challenge after all the work he had done, yet there was something missing. He didn't know what it was, but it didn't seem to hold him back. He ran as hard as he had ever run. He knew he could win.

Ursi felt his speed pull him from the crowd, but he wasn't alone. There was someone on his heels, beating the dirt hard. He stared ahead, never looking back, believing it was the girl from the Windfire Clan.

Ahead, the racing track curved through a gully and beneath a bridge. Ursi followed it easily, never slowing until he reached the bridge. There he noticed a shadow, and glancing up, he saw a small boy on the railing. A rock fell toward him. Ursi didn't waste a second. He jumped aside.

The rock missed him, but Ursi heard a groan. He turned to see the girl from the Windfire Clan sprawled in the dirt with the rock beside her. He bent down. She was still breathing, but her head was bleeding hard. He knew she would die soon if he didn't help her.

Ursi looked behind and saw no runners close to them. He looked ahead and chewed his lip. The race was his. Even the time he lost in stopping could be made up easily. His clan would be proud. Yes, proud he had won and proud that this rock had killed his enemy.

But Ursi couldn't leave her. He was surprised. All at once, he knew what had been missing as he started the race. All his life he had been taught to hate the Windfire People, but now, as he looked inside himself, he found no hate.

Ursi ripped a strip of cloth from his shirt and wrapped it around the wound. It didn't stop the bleeding, so he picked her up.

Then he heard a mournful wail behind him and felt the fists of the small boy beating him hard. "Put her down. Put her down. You killed her. You killed my sister. It should have been you. The rock was for you."

Ursi flinched as he looked at the boy. He knew what would await him back at the start of the race— his father's shame, his clan's anger, and all for what? This boy would not be grateful. No one would, not even the girl in his arms. She would probably hate him more for it.

He felt his legs tremble as he took the first step back. It was hard, very hard. The boy was screaming now, "Put her down, you filthy beast. Put her down."

A runner passed him by, and then another. He flinched again but broke into a trot. Faster and faster, he moved back through the crowd of challengers that swarmed around him.

And then a spasm hit him in the heart and he was free. The runners were gone. The boy was far behind. There was just him and the girl in his arms. Ursi knew she might live if he found a healer soon enough, so Ursi ran as if the girl was Seffalie.

He found a healer's tent set up in the crowd by the starting line. The healer was of a different clan than Ursi or the girl, but he agreed to work on her.

"Will she live?" Ursi asked the old healer as he watched the girl's labored breath.

The old man nodded and glanced at him sideways. "What are you doing helping an enemy?" he asked suspiciously.

Ursi thought a moment and then smiled. "It is the first giving," he answered. "It is the price of freedom."

"Freedom?" the healer questioned him.

"Yes," Ursi said simply.

Ursi slipped from the tent and moved slowly through the crowd, ready to return alone to his mountains and find that path to the cliff. He walked toward the city gates, but as he walked, the crowd seemed to disappear. There were only a few young children playing by the side of the road.

And then it wasn't a road. It was a path—a gentle path that wound between the houses of the city. And then the houses were not houses anymore. They blended into the hills, becoming bushes and rocks and trees. And up ahead, in the distance, he could see a cliff.

Yes. Up ahead, he knew, would be the cliff. And then a time spent in the waiting room, and then...

He stopped a moment. He saw it clearly. There it was—that brown rock glaring in the sun with a split that looked shallow, but was deep.

Yes. There it was, the cliff.

121

Ursi's heart soared as he broke into a run. Faster and faster, he moved over the dry earth until he was standing before the cave in the cliff. Then, gulping a breath, he stepped inside, letting the coolness of the shadows flow over him as he whispered again and again and again, "Seffalie."

Beyond the Star

Long ago, in the Kingdom of the Great Star, a minstrel boy, named Justin, was hunting Fairies of the Wood when he heard a beautiful voice singing in the forest.

Justin peered through the twilight shadows of the trees and saw someone walking beside a stream. "It must be a fairy," he murmured as he crept forward.

Moving from rock to rock and tree to tree, he followed the mysterious figure, listening to the voice. "I know it's a fairy," Justin assured himself, for fairies had magical voices, far lovelier than any human's.

However, the next moment he wasn't so sure. The melody sounded familiar, and a fairy song should be unlike anything he had ever heard. This song reminded him of an old ballad from the Book of Minstrels.

Then, stopping a moment, Justin watched the Great Star rise in the evening sky. The sight of it made him shiver with excitement.

"Soon I'll be like that star," he thought aloud, "Great and brilliant—above everyone else."

He imagined how shocked the other minstrels

125

from his school would be if he won the title of Royal Troubadour. None of them would dare try for it. Justin, however, knew he must go before the king to fulfill that longing for greatness within him.

Noticing the voice in the forest once more, he turned and walked cautiously through the trees. Then, peering around a bramble bush, he saw a cave and a young girl stirring a pot over a small fire as she hummed.

"Good day." He waved as he strode toward her. "Were you singing just now? Your voice is marvelous. I thought you were a fairy."

The girl smiled bashfully.

"My name is Justin." The minstrel bowed. Then he looked at her curiously. "Who are you? What are you doing alone here in the woods?"

"My name is Althea," the girl replied softly, "But I'm not alone. I've a brother, Samuel, who works as a stable boy at the Manor House."

Justin looked beyond the girl into the darkness of the cave. "This is the sort of cave I've been looking for," he told the girl. "A cave like this could hide the fairies."

Althea broke into laughter as delicate as the ringing of a crystal bell. "You won't find any fairies in this cave, or in any cave for that matter," she explained. "The fairies of this forest live within the trees."

"So you've seen the Fairies of the Wood?" Justin asked.

"Not really," said Althea, "But I feel them watching me; and sometimes, when I wake at night, it seems I've heard a fairy song that I can't quite remember."

Justin sat beside the fire to warm his hands. "I would remember," he said. "That's why I've come here. I want to learn the songs of the fairies."

Althea looked at him with amusement and offered him a bowl of oats. He ate it gratefully as she asked him, "What would you do with those fairy songs?"

"I'm going to be the new minstrel for the King," he explained. "I'm the best harpist at my minstrel school, and I know I'm the best in the kingdom. If I learn the songs of the fairies, there is nothing that can stop me being the Royal Troubadour."

"I see," said the girl. Then a chilly autumn wind sprang up, and Althea coughed. She leaned a little closer to the fire and ate her porridge.

Soon there was a snap of a twig, and a tall boy appeared beside the fire.

Althea smiled. "Brother, you're late."

"And so would you be if you had to work for Gregory." Samuel sniffed. "He has a good heart, but every time you finish one job, he remembers another one to be done." Then he turned toward Justin. "Who's this?"

"This is Justin," the girl explained. "He's a minstrel and he's come to learn the songs of the fairies."

"Fairy songs?" Samuel scoffed. "No one ever remembers the song of a fairy."

"I will," said Justin with determination. "I'll wander the woods tonight. I will not sleep. I'll remember if I stay awake."

"Ah, but the music is enchanted," advised Samuel. "It will put you to sleep."

"Not if I keep my eye on the Great Star," Justin whispered. "The Great Star will help me."

Samuel shrugged, then turned to his sister. "Here, Althea, look what Gregory gave me."

Althea's eyes grew wide as her brother held up an old moth-eaten blanket. He wrapped it gently around her shoulders. She hugged him with appreciation.

"I wish it were more," Samuel said.

"It is enough," said Althea.

After Samuel had eaten, Althea went to the stream to wash the dishes. Justin shook his head as he watched her go. "I would never let my sister wear such a rag."

Samuel's head dropped. He stared numbly at his feet.

Justin noticed the shamed look on the boy's face. "I'm sorry," he apologized. "I shouldn't have."

"No," said Samuel. "You're right. Ever since we lost our parents, I've tried to keep her with me, but I just can't earn enough to give her what she needs. The winter's coming, and this cave is damp and cold."

"Couldn't she find a place in the kitchen where you work?" asked Justin gently.

Samuel shook his head. "I've asked and asked, but the only place I've found for her is with an innkeeper a day's journey from here." Tears sprang to Samuel's eyes. "I just can't bear to let her go."

Justin sat silently, not knowing what to say. He watched as Althea came back, clutching the worn blanket to her. She coughed again and sat by the fire to dry her hands.

Samuel cleared his throat. "I've found a place for you, Sister, at an inn. It's not too far away."

"No, Samuel." Althea shook her head. "I'll be fine here. I couldn't leave you."

"But the winter's coming... and the snow." Samuel protested.

Althea touched her brother's arm. "I have a feeling that something will happen. It feels strong and near. Perhaps there will be a place for me at the Manor House soon."

As if to agree with Althea, the fire crackled and popped from the sap sizzling on the wood. The children sat quietly, watching those red-orange flames. Then Justin noticed the Great Star shimmering in the night sky. He rose quietly and said goodbye, striding out into the forest with a heart full of expectation. However, beyond the light of the fire, he found himself a little nervous about the noises of the night.

"I must watch the star," he told himself, "And be brave."

The star pulsed brightly. He watched it faithfully as he made his way over rocks thick with moss and fallen trees higher than his waist. Sometimes the star was hidden by the thick forest canopy, but still he saw its glow and he kept his sights on it.

Finally, he came to a huge tree in the middle of a small clearing. He sat beneath it for a rest, watching the star and telling himself, again and again, how he would shine like it one day. Soon, though, he found his thoughts drifting back to the fire, and the brother and sister who would still be sitting around it.

He thought of the girl, shivering in the cold of the cave, and of the brother that loved her so. Having no family himself, something in the bond he saw between Samuel and Althea touched a longing within him. He found himself wishing that he was their cousin or even a long-lost brother.

As Justin sat in the starlight, he tried to think of a way he might help them stay together. He imagined finding work for both of them in one place or another, like an inn near the royal castle. And then he realized, as the Royal Troubadour, he could invite them to come live in the castle of the King. He could say they were his family.

A wind stirred the branches of the oak. Justin sat up abruptly, knowing it was more important than ever to find the fairies. Now his quest wasn't just for him, it was for Althea and Samuel.

He looked around him. Althea had told him the fairies lived within the trees. He touched the wood of the great oak beside him. Certainly, this tree should have a fairy or two within it, but how could he find them?

Justin thought a moment as he studied the bark. Perhaps there was a door, and if he touched the right knob or knothole or branch, it would open. Carefully, he felt and prodded around the whole tree, but had no success.

Finally, Justin decided to hide and watch for fairies near the tree. He walked away, as if he was leaving, then doubled back toward the clearing and hid behind a bush. He crouched low and waited.

A long time passed. Justin's eyes grew heavy. To keep alert, he looked up at the Great Star and thought of Samuel and Althea. Finally, something near the tree caught his eye.

He saw a tall shape filled with light. It glided, more than walked; and as it approached the tree it sang a note, clear and high. Part of the tree moved. Suddenly, the oak was shimmering as if a door had opened and moonlight spilled out into the night.

Justin watched the doorway close silently behind

the figure. Then he crept forward and stood before the oak, listening. He couldn't hear a sound, but he knew what to do. He sang that note, clear and loud, that the fairy had sung.

Very quietly, the doorway opened, and Justin stood before a tree-lined path that sparkled magically. The trees were tall—taller even than the giant oak that held them. They shimmered silver in the night.

Justin looked along the path. It was empty, so he stepped through the door and crept along it. In the distance, he could hear the sound of voices singing. Eagerly, he crept closer. Then, all at once, he could see a glade where Fairies of the Wood danced and sang to the music of a golden harp.

Justin stared at them in amazement. They were a giant race of tree-like fairies, taller than Justin by three or perhaps four times. Their eyes blazed with a green fire, like emeralds all aglow. They wore cloaks of silver leaves and had no wings, for they were of the forest and didn't need to fly.

Justin slipped behind a tree and listened to the fairies' songs. Some songs were lively, others slow and restful, but all of them were beautiful and elusive. Justin found it difficult to remember the notes and rhythms, which were so strange to him; but with the heart of a great musician, he listened for what seemed like half the night.

Finally, he turned to go, slipping back down the

132

fairy pathway. However, as he reached the door, it opened. A giant fairy stood before him, watching him with those emerald eyes.

"Sit down," said the fairy, "And I will sing to you."

It was then that Justin realized how weary he was. His concentration on the songs had kept him awake, but now he knew he could forget them all, in an instant, if he fell asleep. And if he fell asleep, the fairies within the tree would only seem like a dream when he woke. So he looked wildly about him for the Great Star, but in the fairy kingdom there were no stars in the sky.

"I will not listen until I see the stars," Justin said firmly.

"Very well," said the fairy. She stepped clear of the doorway, but would not let him pass through it. "Sit here and listen and watch the stars."

Justin sat so he could see the Great Star, and the fairy began to sing. It was the most beautiful song he'd heard that night and the most enchanted. Each verse seemed to have a slightly different melody, and as he watched the star, his mind drifted close to sleep.

"I cannot see the stars very well from here," Justin interrupted. "Let me sit in the night air and see them above me."

"Very well," said the fairy, "But do not run away. These are our woods, and the beasts of the night will hear me call if you run."

So Justin stepped into the frosty night, and the chill of the air woke him. He sat beneath the oak and stared hard at the Great Star, which was low on the horizon. Justin knew, if he could stay awake a little longer, the sun would rise.

The fairy sang softly, like a mother to a child to help it sleep. Somehow, Justin managed to stay alert, thinking of Samuel and Althea and what must be done; but he wasn't sure how long he could fight off his weariness.

Then, all at once, the fairy stopped. She touched Justin with her shimmering hand and said, "The sun will rise soon, and if you can tell me what is beyond that star you watch, I will let you keep the memory of this night and leave you in peace."

Justin sat up. "Beyond the star? Beyond the Great Star?"

He stared at its brightness and tried to look past it. All he could see was its great light. He shrugged. "Nothing," he replied.

"Think," said the fairy, "If you can see beyond the star, then you will understand enough to remember all you've seen."

Justin searched his mind for some clue to the secret behind the star. However, all that would come to him was Althea's voice singing in the woods. Over and over, he remembered the song she had sung. It

134

occurred to him that he wished he had asked her to sing another one. Her voice was beautiful, like a gift of magic. There was something pure about it, something brilliant, something radiant as a star.

And then a sweat broke out on Justin's forehead. He stared at the Great Star. His body trembled with a knowing that came as a great shock. He tried to forget it, but he couldn't shake loose of it. He had always thought of himself as being great like the star, but now he knew the greatness wasn't in him. He could play the harp well, and his voice was sweet, but it wasn't pure. In that instant, he knew Althea was the star, and it was she that should be singing for the King.

Justin stared at the fairy. "I've been so wrong," he said in disbelief.

"Yes." The fairy nodded. "You understand a little more, yet you still cannot see beyond the star." Then she touched his eyes and sung to him, and he drifted into sleep.

Justin woke in the bright sunlight at the prodding of a hand. He looked up into the face of Althea, then shook himself. A vague dream clouded his mind. There was a face with emerald eyes, a starless sky within the oak, and many songs he couldn't quite remember. The only thing clear to him was that he longed to see beyond the Great Star.

Then he realized Althea was speaking to him in

earnest. "I have a song for you," she was saying, "A song of the fairies."

"What song?" Justin mumbled, his mind still heavy with sleep.

"A fairy song—a gift from the fairies," Althea answered. "It's for you to take to the King."

Justin shook himself, trying to understand. Suddenly he stood up, realizing he had fallen asleep and forgotten all the fairy songs. "They're gone," he cried in despair. "I've lost all the songs."

"No they're not," Althea insisted. "I have one for you."

"A fairy song? But how?"

"They came to me in early morning, just before dawn," Althea said breathlessly. "They woke me and took me out from the cave to see the stars. Their eyes were as beautiful as emeralds, and they pointed to the Great Star, asking me if I could see what lay beyond it."

"That was it!" Justin shouted. "That was the question I couldn't answer. Could you?"

"Yes." Althea smiled. "I told them that beyond the star was the sky."

"The sky?" Justin frowned.

"Yes," explained Althea, "Everything in the heavens—the moon, the blackness of the night and the lesser stars, too." Althea swept her hand above her in a grand gesture. "Everything." She turned and smiled at him. "Then they gave me this song."

Althea grabbed his hand and stared into his eyes. She sang, in her pure, clear voice, a song so wonderful and mysterious Justin could hardly bear to listen. A shiver went up his spine. Tears flowed to his eyes. Then he saw, in his mind's eye, Althea sitting for the King, singing again and again the song of the fairies.

"Althea," he said softly when she'd finished, "You must come and sing that for the King. You'll win the honor of being his troubadour."

Althea flushed and shook her head. "No! No!" she protested.

"You must," Justin argued.

"But I know so few songs and I can't even play the harp," Althea stammered, "And a girl has never been the Royal Troubadour."

"I'll teach you all that," said Justin. "And it doesn't matter if you're a girl. You have a gift that's truly as great as the star."

Althea looked around, bewildered and afraid. Justin squeezed her hand and whispered, "I'll be there with you. I'll buy you a dress and a cloak and some ribbons for your hair. You can't refuse now. You've been given a gift from the fairies."

"You'll stay with me?" Althea asked hesitantly. "And Samuel too?"

"Yes," said Justin. "For as long as you command us to."

"And that would be forever," Althea replied as Justin smiled gratefully.

Then they sat beneath the clear autumn sky while golden oak leaves fell around them. Once again, Althea sang the song of the fairies.

And while she sang, Justin looked up at the blue above him, finally understanding the answer Althea had given to the fairies. There were no stars, now, only the sky. Yet within the sky, hidden by that covering of blue, there was the Great Star and also fainter stars—but none of them mattered in the daylight.

He knew, now, what the fairy had asked of him. Just yesterday, he could only see the Great Star. It had been so important to him, but it was only part of the sky as he was only part of the forest or the kingdom.

All at once, a peace swept over him as he listened to Althea. Now, he didn't need to shine above all else. It was as if he had reached beyond the star to become the sky, and he was one with everything in it.

Then Althea stopped singing. She touched Justin softly on the hand as she said, "I will sing for the King if you will play the harp along side of me. You have a gift, too, to share."

Justin smiled. He took his harp from his pack and plucked it gently. He nodded. "Yes, Althea. I will."

Then they sat in silence, not needing to move or

138

speak. Justin felt the sunshine warm his face. The smell of oak leaves were clear and strong. And somewhere within the gnarled trunk of the oak, he thought he caught a glimpse, just for a second, of a fairy filled with light, watching them with eyes like emeralds.

The Clock of Nalaba

Far, far away, high between the peaks of the Nalaba Mountains, there once lived a clockmaker named Tally Malloon. He lived so far from the cities and farms in the valleys below that the clockmaker barely had any customers come to his door. Yet Tally was always busy, for he was the keeper of the Clock of Nalaba.

Deep in a cavern, below the house where Tally lived, was the giant Clock of Nalaba. It lay flat, like a sundial would, among the limestone columns of the cave. Its black iron hands swept, minute by minute and hour by hour, above its golden face. And though it was beautiful, only the keeper and his family ever saw the clock, for it was guarded by spells of magic.

Long ago, the Clock of Nalaba had been set into the floor of the cavern by a power as old as time itself. No one knew who had built the clock, but the wizards and sorcerers of the land warned against its destruction. It was even written, in the ancient Legend of Nalaba, that without the clock's steady tick, tick, tick time would stop.

141

Twice each day, at twelve o'clock, Tally took two large keys from the wall of his workshop and went down to the cavern to wind the great clock. First he would unlock the door to the cavern with the long key and descend the iron stairs. Next he would open up the glass case covering the clock with the short, wide one. After a brisk walk over the clock face, he would come to its center and use the short, wide key to wind the clock twelve turns. Twelve turns, one for each hour, that was all.

Now, Tally Malloon had a wife and two daughters. One daughter was just a baby, but the other one was a tall, strong girl named Mitty. Every day, at noon, Mitty would beg for a chance to wind the clock, and every day her father would shake his head no.

"It's a mighty important job to wind the ancient clock," Tally Malloon would explain gravely to his daughter as he unlocked the door to the cavern. "That clock is the source of all time, and it's my job to see it is wound properly."

Mitty would sigh and watch from the top of the stair as her father wound the clock. Then, when he took his afternoon nap, she would slip into the workshop, take the keys off the wall and sneak down into the cavern, alone, to admire the magical clock.

Mitty never tried to wind the clock herself. That had to be done at just the right time or the clock might be broken. What she did, instead, was to walk across the glass case above those metal hands and sit right in the very center of the clock. It was there, in the center, that time disappeared, and Mitty felt like she was floating through eternity.

Mitty liked that timeless feeling. It made her a little dizzy until she focused on it completely. Then it became a great openness where her thoughts were gone. The only thing left was a stillness, spreading outward farther than she could imagine. And though she only sat for a few minutes on the clock, it seemed like forever.

Life went on like this for a long time until Mitty was twelve. By then, she was so used to sitting in the center of the clock without time, that she began to have that timeless feeling at odd moments around the house or out in the yard. It wouldn't stay for very long, but Mitty would always smile as the moment came and passed, for it left her feeling very, very peaceful.

One summer's day, Mitty was stacking wood in the woodshed when she drifted into that peaceful, eternal feeling. This time it didn't fade. So, piece by piece and step by step, she carried firewood from the pile in the yard to the little stone shed. Moment by moment, she stacked the logs neatly in long rows inside the shed. She didn't think of anything. She just worked without wondering when the job would end.

Suddenly, the job was done. She looked around

143

herself and blinked. "Oh, this is wonderful!" Mitty said, feeling happy and calm and not tired at all. "I should do everything this way."

So Mitty spent all day cooking and cleaning and scrubbing in the stillness beyond time. Then, when her work was done, she sat under a tree and hummed softly to some rabbits in the meadow. The tune was one she had never heard before, for she had let go of all the songs she ever knew. Each note came to her as she sang, and the rabbits gathered around to hear the beautiful melody that changed with each new moment.

"I wish there wasn't time at all," Mitty said to the rabbits when she finally stopped singing. "I wish I could always live this way, moment by moment."

The rabbits wiggled their noses enthusiastically as if they really understood. Then they hopped off to the trees beyond the meadow, not caring to listen anymore. Mitty laughed, for that's how things came and went in the timelessness.

Later that night, as her father tucked her in bed, Mitty looked at a wishing star on the horizon and wondered, "What would the world be like if there was no time?"

Tally Malloon looked at his daughter curiously. "Why do you ask?"

Mitty squirmed under her blankets, knowing she couldn't tell him her secret about sitting in the center of the clock. "Because..." she mumbled, "Because I wonder what would happen if the clock broke."

"The clock won't break, you can be sure of that," Tally said firmly. "But... if there was no time, why then I guess the world would stop."

"Stop?" Mitty asked.

"Yes, stop," Tally answered with a nod. "Probably just from the shock of it."

Mitty shook her head. "But why? I don't understand."

"People are used to time," her father explained. "They're used to having today, tomorrow, and yesterday. If time stopped, they wouldn't know how to think or what to do."

"But what about the plants and the birds and the sun and the moon? Would everything stop?" Mitty wondered.

"Maybe," her father said. "Or maybe it would just seem like it stopped. I don't know. There wouldn't be any way to tell. There would just be one moment, the now, and no way to remember what it was like before."

"I see," said Mitty slowly. "But couldn't people get used to it?"

Tally Malloon laughed and kissed his daughter goodnight. "It would take a lot of practice, but people could get used to it."

Then Mitty sighed and closed her eyes and fell asleep into dreamy timelessness.

The very next day a stranger came to the clockmaker's door. Tally Malloon invited him in, but the dark, cloaked man declined. He looked over his shoulder with a wary eye and whispered, "I've just come to warn you there's a goblin on the loose. It's an ugly shadow of a creature named Nailbreath. Eats metal, it does, the little beast. Tore down a whole house, it did, just to get the nails."

Tally laughed. "A nail-eating goblin? I never heard of one."

"I laughed too," said the man grimly, "Until it ate my sword and sheath and armor while I slept. I'm a knight by trade. I need my sword to fight. Now I won't rest till I find that thing and teach it a lesson. They say a bucket of water will rust its insides good and give it indigestion."

Tally Malloon chuckled and wished the fellow well. Then he closed the door, smiling at Mitty. "Never heard of such a thing," he said.

"Oh, Father," said Mitty, "I wouldn't laugh. Just think of all the clocks in your workshop it could eat."

Her father scratched his head and nodded. "That's true, Mitty. We'll keep the door locked tight." Then her father went upstairs for his nap, leaving Mitty to guard the door.

Mitty stayed up late that night, worried that a goblin who ate metal couldn't be stopped by an iron bolt on the door. It was almost midnight when she banked the fire and crept upstairs to her bed. Then, as soon as she had settled, her mother came in and shook her.

"Mitty, wake up. Your father's ill. He wants you to wind the clock."

Mitty sat up in shock. "Wind the clock?" she asked, "He wants me to wind the clock?"

"Yes, yes," whispered her mother. "Now hurry. It's almost midnight."

Trembling with excitement, Mitty lit a candle and went back down the stairs to the workshop door. She pushed it open and shone the candle against the wall to the spot where the huge keys hung. However, to her surprise, the wooden hook that held the keys was empty. She looked around, in horror, to find the whole workshop torn apart with clocks strewn everywhere.

As she shone her light toward the corner of the workshop, she caught sight of a strange shadow with glowing red eyes. She heard the jangle of the missing keys and a wicked chuckle as the shadow leapt past her across the room.

"Stop!" she yelled as she chased the goblin, but it ran through the front room and disappeared beyond the cottage door into the night. Mitty turned and called up the stairs, "The goblin! Mother! Father! The goblin!"

"Hush! Hush!" her mother whispered as she crept down the stairs. "Your father's ill, remember?"

"But the keys are gone. The goblin has them," Mitty cried. "I can not wind the clock."

147

"Oh, dear," said her mother, "And it's almost midnight."

"What happens if the clock's not wound at midnight?" Mitty asked fearfully.

"I don't know." Her mother wrung her hands. "I think it stops."

Just then, Mitty turned to see the clock on the mantel strike midnight. It rang one tremor of a chime and grew silent. Mitty waited for the other eleven chimes, but they never came. Then she noticed the fire had stopped flickering and her mother was terribly still.

"What's happening?" Mitty asked, but she already knew. Along with the clock, time had stopped. There was no past, no future—only the moment of now, only timelessness.

And then Mitty realized she was frozen with time like her mother. When time had stopped, so had everything else, just like her father said.

Yet, even as she stood there stiff as a statue, she knew yesterday she had worked and sang beyond the bonds of time. If she could do that now, she might be able to find the key to the clock. She focused on that stillness within her, imagining herself in the center of the magic clock. All at once, that timeless feeling filled her, and she found she could move again.

Without hesitation, she stepped through the front door, noticing for one brief moment that, indeed, the goblin had nibbled through the lock. Then that thought slipped away forever as she stared at the full moon. The moon glowed around her, illuminating the night. It was beautiful; but there was no wind, no noise, no sign of life anywhere. Mitty knew, without time, she was the only person in the world that moved—perhaps the only living thing.

That thought would have frozen her with fear if she hadn't let it slip away. In the fresh moment that came, her only thought was to find the keys and wind the clock.

And even that thought she let go of as she stepped onto the path into the darkness. She didn't know where to look, and if she paused to think about it, it would stop her there in the moonlight. So she pushed away all thoughts, having faith in the moment, and let the openness within her be her guide.

Mitty wandered, moment by moment, along the mountain trails. Then, all at once, she found the knight hiding in a bush with a bucket of water in his hands. Before him was the goblin sitting on a rock. It was frozen, too, with its teeth clenched tight on the short, wide key that wound the Clock of Nalaba.

Reaching for the set of keys, she gave them a yank, but they were stuck in the goblin's mouth. Then she stood absolutely still, staring at the goblin, wondering what to do.

There were a thousand things she could have

tried to free the keys from the goblin's mouth. Ideas raced through her like lightning bolts. However, in the end, she just cleared her mind, waiting for something within her to act. All at once, she reached out and yanked even harder on the keys. The goblin fell off the rock with a noiseless, timeless crash.

She rolled the goblin over to find the keys had broken free in the fall. She picked them up and smiled at the funny creature, remembering what the knight had said about rusting up its insides with a bucket of water. She wished, as she walked away, that she could see the knight pouring that water down the goblin's mouth. However, remembering and wishing brought her out of timelessness and slowed her down, so she released those thoughts to be one with the moment again.

Moment by moment, she made her way back to the great Clock of Nalaba. Then she stood before it, opening its case with the short, wide key that now had a small bite out of it. Step by step, she crossed the face of the clock and slid the key into the round hole for winding. Slowly, she wound the clock once, twice, thrice. Then, before she pushed against the key to turn it for the fourth time, something made her stop.

Mitty stood blankly for a moment. She realized that twelve turns of the key might be too many. Perhaps, to get time started properly, she should compensate for whatever time was lost. Yet, how could she ever know how many turns were needed to make time right again?

It was the one time when Mitty's faith in the moment faltered. She let go of the key and stepped back from the center of the clock face. Suddenly she was frozen, motionless, at the tip of the black minute hand of the clock. Her thoughts raced, and her fears grew, and she lost her hope of winding the clock.

She struggled for what seemed like forever to get back into timelessness, but the struggle only kept her from it. Then, like a clear bell ringing through her mind, a voice said, "Do nothing. Relax. Do nothing. I will wind the clock."

She relaxed. She could turn. She could see her father coming toward her across the clock. "But how can you?... How do you know?... How can you move when time has stopped?" Mitty sputtered.

All at once, he was beside her. He reached out, rumpling her hair gently. "And you think it's only you who knows the secret of the Clock of Nalaba?" he asked with a wink. "I was younger than you were, was I, when I first discovered the center of the clock."

Then he went to the key in the center and closed his eyes, turning it for the fourth and the fifth and almost the sixth time. "There," he said, "That's enough. I can feel it. That's enough."

Mitty grinned and stepped clear as the big minute hand jumped forward one tick. Time had begun again.

Suddenly, there was a clatter on the stairs as Mitty's mother came running. She looked at the clockmaker with alarm. "What are you doing out of bed?"

"Just helping Mitty wind the clock," he said with a chuckle. "I feel much better, too." He kissed his wife affectionately; then he picked up the key, pointing to the bitten edge. "What's this?" he cried.

"The goblin took a little taste of it," Mitty explained. "However," she added with a smile, "I don't think he'll be bothering us again for a very long time."

She told them of her adventure with the goblin and of the knight who was probably, at this very moment, pouring water down its throat.

"Never heard of such a thing," her father laughed. "A key-eating goblin." He turned to his daughter with a twinkle in his eye and added, "I think it's time you had your own set of keys to the clock, don't you?"

"Yes, Father." Mitty smiled proudly. "It's time."

Then they closed the case and went upstairs and locked the door to the Clock of Nalaba.

ABOUT THE AUTHOR:

"These stories are like visions I long to see as I look ahead down the pathway of my growth," says Arlene Williams who lives in Sparks, Nevada with her husband and two children. She has been writing since 1979 and has been a student of *The Course in Miracles* since 1983. These two passions in her life have merged to produce *FAIRY TALES FOR THE NEW AGE* – her second book for children.

ABOUT THE ILLUSTRATOR:

"Children's book illustrating is a wonderful challenge," says Joyce Rossi. "You have to listen very carefully to the story and let it tell you what the pictures should be. Getting those images down on paper using sound composition and appropriate technique are all part of an exciting puzzle. When all the pieces fit together just right...what a joy!"

Joyce teaches six classes a week to children and adults in her home studio and is also the owner of a freelance graphic design business. She and her husband Lou, live in Verdi, Nevada with their two sons, Vince and Mike.